Microcomputers and DOS

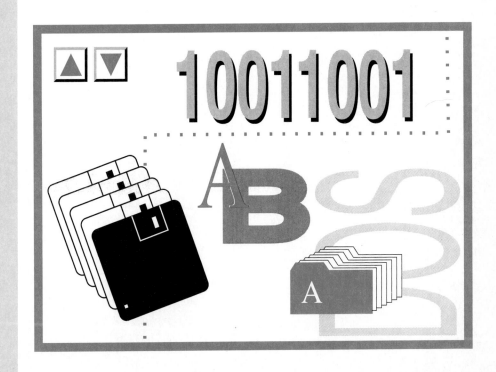

Microcomputers and DOS: A Short Course

Dennis P. Curtin

REGENTS/PRENTICE HALL
Englewood Cliffs, New Jersey 07632

Library of Congress Cataloging-in-Publication Data
Curtin, Dennis P.
    Microcomputers and DOS: a short course / Dennis P. Curtin.
        p.   cm. — (Computer application software series)
    Rev. ed. of: DOS, a short course. ©1990.
    Includes index.
    ISBN 0-13-584830-X (paper)
        1. Microcomputers. 2. MS-DOS (Computer file) 3. PC-DOS (Computer
file) I. Curtin, Dennis P., DOS, a short course.
II. Title. III. Series.
QA76.5.C796 1993
004.16—dc20   92-8684
                                                    CIP

Acquisitions editor: Liz Kendall
Editorial/production supervision: Cecil Yarbrough
Copy editor: Robert Fiske
Designer and half-title illustrator: Janis Owens
Cover designer: Marianne Frasco
Interior art production: Dennis P. Curtin
Desktop publishing: Cathleen Morin
Prepress buyer: Ilene Levy
Manufacturing buyer: Ed O'Dougherty
Supplements editor: Cindy Harford
Editorial assistant: Jane Avery

Cover art: Compass dial printed from a copper plate
made by Samuel Emery of Salem, Massachusetts (1809-1882),
by permission of the Peabody Museum of Salem

© 1993 by REGENTS/PRENTICE HALL
A Division of Simon & Schuster
Englewood Cliffs, New Jersey 07632

Printed in the United States of America
10 9 8 7 6 5 4 3 2

ISBN 0-13-584830-X

Prentice-Hall International (UK) Limited, *London*
Prentice-Hall of Australia Pty. Limited, *Sydney*
Prentice-Hall of Canada Inc., *Toronto*
Prentice-Hall Hispanoamericana, S.A., *Mexico*
Prentice-Hall of India Private Limited, *New Delhi*
Prentice-Hall of Japan, Inc., *Tokyo*
Simon & Schuster Asia Ptd. Ltd., *Singapore*
Editora Prentice-Hall do Brasil, Ltda., *Rio de Janeiro*

C O N T E N T S

CONTENTS

Do You Need Incentive?
Workers who use computers but are similar in every other respect to workers who do not earn a fat bonus of 10 to 15 percent for their knack with these machines.
The New York Times, *February 14, 1992, page D2, referring to a study by Alan B. Krueger of Princeton University.*

ASK THE AUTHOR

Dennis Curtin welcomes your questions about his textbooks and hardware and software issues. Please feel free to call him at 1-800-926-7074. For examination copies or ordering issues, call your Regents/ Prentice Hall representative.

Q U I E T !!
R E F E R E N C E
S E C T I O N

This text introduces you to microcomputers and the operating system known as DOS. DOS has been revised over the years, and this text covers all versions up to DOS 5, the version introduced in 1992. As you proceed through the text, you will learn all of the basic concepts and procedures you need to understand in order to operate a computer. To simplify your introduction as much as possible, the text is organized into topics and chapters.

Topics: The Basic Unit

The basic unit of this text is the topic, a short section that is narrowly focused on a specific part of the computer or a specific DOS procedure. This narrow focus, and the precise beginning and end of a topic, make it easier for you to study than does a traditional chapter organization. Short topics are less intimidating than long chapters, and they make it easier for your instructor to assign specific sections.

The first five topics introduce the microcomputer and devices such as keyboards, display monitors, and printers. The remaining topics introduce the disk operating system. Each of the topics on DOS contains the following elements:

- *Objectives* tell you what you should be able to accomplish when you have finished the topic.
- *Introductory concepts* introduce the basic principles discussed in the topic. These concepts all apply to DOS, but many also apply to other programs you will eventually use on a microcomputer. When you understand concepts, procedures are easier to learn because they fit into a framework. Understanding concepts also makes it much easier to transfer your understanding to other programs and other computers.
- *Tutorials* demonstrate step by step how to use the procedures discussed in the topic. If you follow the instructions, you quickly see how each procedure is performed and the results it has. This establishes a framework on which you can hang a better understanding of the procedures that are discussed in detail in the section that follows.
- The *Quick Reference* describes step by step how you execute commands. This section serves a dual function: You can refer to it when working on the activities in this text or when working on your own projects. Many of the procedures are presented step by step in highlighted KEY/Strokes boxes.
- *Exercises* provide you with additional opportunities to practice and gain experience with the concepts and procedures discussed in the topic. Unlike tutorials, the exercises do not guide you step by step. You have to determine the correct procedures to use.

Chapters: A Pause for Reinforcement

Related topics are grouped into chapters so you can pause to review and test yourself. At the end of each chapter are the following sections you should complete:

- A review of the key concepts and procedures that were discussed in the chapter.
- A series of questions that test your understanding of the concepts and procedures discussed in the chapter. There are three types of questions: fill in the blank, match the columns, and write out the answer.
- Projects that build skills and introduce problem solving. Background material is provided for each project, but no specific procedures are given. To complete the projects, you must already have mastered the topics in the chapter or go back and look up the information that you need.

Hands-On Lab Activities

In a lab-oriented course, your progress and enjoyment are highly dependent on the quality of the hands-on activities used as vehicles to teach you concepts and procedures. Ideally, these hands-on activities perform a number of useful functions.

- They build skills in the specific procedures you need to know.
- They demonstrate a variety of situations in which specific procedures are useful.
- They develop problem-solving skills. Exercises provide less guidance for you than tutorials, and projects provide even less. Moving though this sequence of activities challenges you to think about what you should do and why you need to do it.

This text includes dozens of such activities and presents them on three levels: tutorials, exercises, and projects. Each level requires an increasingly better understanding of DOS to complete it successfully.

- Tutorials introduce a specific procedure or a group of closely related procedures. Their purpose is to demonstrate how the procedures work and show the effects they have.
- Exercises at the end of each topic reinforce the concepts and procedures discussed in the topic. They focus on the topic of which they are a part. You will have to rely on your experience with the tutorial and refer to the Quick Reference section to find the information you need to complete exercises. This refines your ability to look up information you need to complete tasks—something you will have to do on your own when the class is over.
- Projects at the end of each chapter are like exercises, but require an understanding of more than one topic to complete them.

Key Features

This text has a number of features that distinguish it from other texts in this area.

- *A Jump-Start tutorial* is in Topic 6 so you can begin working on the computer from the very first day that you begin your study of DOS. This tutorial is designed to give you an idea of how the program works and demonstrate some of the things it can do.

JUMP-START TUTORIAL

As the author of many books on computer applications, I teach teachers in seminars and workshops all over the country. If the room has computers, teachers are already punching keys while I'm still giving the introduction. Just like students, they can't wait to do something. The computer is an enticing, interactive tool, not a passive device you just read about. To encourage this hands-on flavor, the first DOS topic in this text (Topic 6) begins with a Jump-Start tutorial that lets you work with the computer and DOS as soon as possible. This tutorial not only lets you begin sooner but also shows you what the operating system can do.

Student Resource Disks
Many of the files on which you work are on the *Student Resource Disk* which your instructor will make available to you.

■ You will find that you first use this text to structure your learning and then later as a reference. To improve the text's usefulness as a reference, most procedures are presented step by step in highlighted KEY/Strokes boxes. By referring to the list of topics on the back cover, you can immediately locate a topic of interest and then skim the Quick Reference section in that topic for the information that you need.

■ At the back of the text is a cardboard punch-out *pocket guide* for DOS.

Getting Ready

Before proceeding with the activities in this text, consider these points:

■ You work only with files on a floppy disk. If your system has a hard disk drive, you use the DOS files stored on it, but you do not work with any of your own files on the hard drive. Making mistakes while doing so could cause problems on your system.

■ Occasionally, you will find references to "floppy disk systems" and "hard disk systems" in this text. By "floppy disk systems" we mean systems on which you run DOS from one floppy disk drive and save your work on a second. By "hard disk systems" we mean any system with DOS on the hard disk drive and at least one floppy disk drive.

■ DOS is published by Microsoft, and, as noted, it has been revised a number of times over the years. Moreover, a number of slightly different versions have also been produced for computer companies such as IBM and Compaq. Depending on which of these numerous revisions and different versions you are using, you may find that the prompts appearing on your screen vary slightly from those discussed in this text. If that happens, just be sure to read the screen carefully and proceed as instructed. In most, if not all cases, these variations will be minor and easily manageable.

The COMPASS Series

This text is part of the COMPASS (Computer Application Software Series) series. In addition to this text there are companion texts covering WordPerfect, Lotus 1-2-3, and dBASE. If your course covers only some of these programs, you can use these separate texts. If your course covers all of these programs, you may want to use the combined volume, *Application Software*, 3rd edition. As these application programs are updated by their publishers and as new programs become more widely used in college courses, new titles are added to the COMPASS series and alternate versions of the combined *Application Software* are released. Contact your local REGENTS/PRENTICE-HALL representative for a current list of the titles available in this series.

Supplements

The publisher has developed many supplements for this text that are free to instructors on adoption. These supplements include:

■ *Instructor's Manual with Tests and Resource Disks* by Donna M. Matherly contains suggested course outlines for a variety of course lengths and formats, chapter summaries, teaching tips for each topic, competencies to be attained, solutions and answers to

in-text activities, competency production tests, a test bank of objective questions, and a number of supplementary problems.

Two types of disks are included with this supplement, and both are available as either 3.5" or 5.25" disks.

- *Student Resource Disk* contains the unformatted files to be used to complete the hands-on activities in this text. This master disk can be duplicated for students. Arrangements can be made to have the *Student Resource Disk* bound to copies of this text for an additional fee—contact your REGENTS/PRENTICE-HALL representative to make arrangements.
- *Instructor's Resource Disk* contains files for chapter summaries, competencies, topic goals and tips, solutions for hands-on activities, competency tests, and supplementary problems.

■ *Course Outlines on Disk* contains files and other information from the Instructor's Manual which allow the professor to customize lecture outlines and course syllabi with ease.

■ Transparencies illustrate essential screen displays for DOS and Windows.

■ *Test Manager* (3.5" and 5.25" disks) is a test-generating package that allows professors to customize the test questions contained in the Instructor's Manual. Users can edit, add to, and scramble test questions.

■ A video covering DOS (Video Professor) is available to qualified adopters.

Acknowledgments

No book is the result of the efforts of a single person, and that is especially true of this text, where many people, from classroom instructors to printers, went the extra mile to create the best possible text. Although I accept full responsibility for any of the text's shortcomings, full credit for the things that were done correctly belongs to others.

The following teachers took time out of their busy schedules and traveled to another state to sit down with me in an all-day session. At that meeting they laid out a plan for me to follow to create the best possible revision of this text:

■ Richard Bernardin, Cape Cod Community College
■ Catherine Brotherton, Riverside Community College
■ Linda Dowell, St. Johns River Community College
■ Nancy P. Houston, Grove City College
■ Sarah J. MacArthur
■ James A. Pope, Old Dominion University
■ Howard Pullman, Youngstown State University
■ Frederick L. Wells, DeKalb College at Gwinnett Center
■ Toni M. Hutto, Wake Technical Community College

A number of people reviewed the outline and/or the final manuscript with care and attention that the author had not previously seen. Many of these instructors spent days reading the manuscript and sharing their insights with the author. Their efforts often required that I reorganize and rewrite major sections of the text; and the final text has been greatly improved as a result.

■ Nancy M. Acree, University of Puget Sound
■ Richard Bernardin, Cape Cod Community College

- Catherine Brotherton, Riverside Community College
- Bruce Case, Thomas Jefferson High School
- Lee D. Cornell, Mankato State University
- Linda Dowell, St. Johns River Community College
- Deborah Haseltine, State Technical Institute at Memphis
- Dennis R. Heckman, Portland Community College
- Toni M. Hutto, Wake Technical Community College
- Donal Janes, Los Medanos College
- Donna M. Matherly, Tallahassee Community College
- Elise S. Patterson-Crate, Florida Community College
- James A. Pope, Old Dominion University
- Bonnie M. Skelton, Radford University
- Donna Yoder, Pima Community College

I would also like to express my appreciation to many others who helped me implement the plan for this text. The supplements that accompany this text were prepared by Donna Matherly. Her work expands on, and improves upon, the content of this text and she is a joy to work with. Robert Fiske and Donna Matherly tested all of the tutorials, exercises, and projects. They tried to chase down every error in concept or keystroke, and any that remain are not a result of their efforts.

Thanks also to all of those at REGENTS/PRENTICE HALL who brought the final result into print. Cecil Yarbrough coordinated all aspects of the book's production and worked as hard as anyone has ever worked to make it the best possible text. His efforts are greatly appreciated and are vividly illustrated in all aspects of this text. Liz Kendall helped plan the revision, coordinated all aspects of the project's development, and encouraged me over long months of writing and rewriting. Liz's assistant, Jane Avery, successfully juggled all of the reviewing and author contacts to keep information flowing well at all times. Without fail, when something was needed it was there. Cathy Morin electronically published the manuscript and worked side by side with me, laying out the pages and suggesting many improvements along the way.

Finally, this book is dedicated to Matthew Dennis Morin, who entertained (or distracted) me as much as possible during its development. His older sister, Emily, took over entertaining and distracting me, when Matt was too tired to continue.

Dennis P. Curtin
Marblehead, Massachusetts

NOTATION USED IN QUICK REFERENCE COMMANDS

In this text, you will occasionally find notations such as **COPY A:**<*filename.ext*>**B:** or **REN** <*oldname.ext*> <*newname.ext*>. The names in brackets indicate the data that you should enter in your own commands. Substitute your own filenames for the brackets and the text within them. For example, if you see **COPY A:**<*filename.ext*>**B:**, enter **COPY A:MYFILE.WP5 B:**. If you see **REN** <*oldname.ext*> <*newname.ext*>, enter **REN JUMPSTRT.WP5 MYFILE.WP5**.

This text uses the following conventions for commands and prompts:

Commands

All keys you press (except those in boxes such as [Enter ←] and all characters you type are shown in the typeface used here for **FILENAME**.

■ Keys you press in sequence are separated by commas. For example, if you are to press [Y], release it, and press [Enter ←], the instructions read [Y], [Enter ←].

■ Keys you press simultaneously are separeted by dashes. For example, if you are to hold down [Ctrl] while you press [PrtScr], the instructions read [Ctrl]-[PrtScr].

Prompts

All prompts, messages, and menu choices are shown *in this typeface*. When a prompt appears, read it carefully and do as it says.

Summary

Now that you have read about how keys and commands are presented, see if you can understand the following instructions:

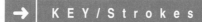

→ **K E Y / S t r o k e s**

To List the Files on a Disk

1. Insert the disk with the files to be listed into the drive.
2. Type *DIR* <drive:> and press [Enter ←].

To follow these instructions, you begin by inserting the disk with the files to be listed into one of the disk drives. If you insert the disk into drive A, you then type the command **DIR A:** and press [Enter ←]. If you insert the disk into drive B, you would type **DIR B:** and press [Enter ←].

Microcomputers and DOS

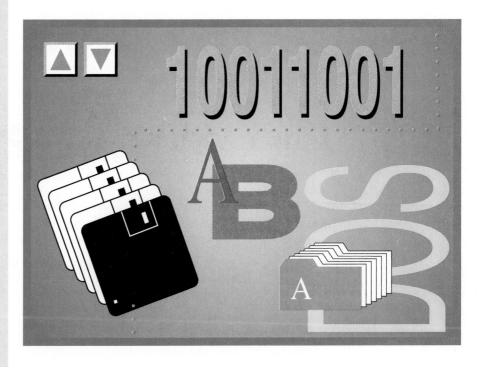

The Computer System

The Digital Revolution

After completing this topic, you will be able to:
- Explain the concepts behind the term *digital*
- Describe how information is stored, processed, and communicated in a computer
- Explain the difference between a bit and a byte

A single concept, called *digital processing*, makes possible the computer and many other modern electronic devices such as compact disc players. Digital processing simply refers to a way information—be it music, numbers, words, or images—is stored, processed, and used.

The term *digital* comes from the word *digit*, which means a single number. When you write a check or count your change, you use the digits 0 through 9. For example, the digits 1 and 9 can convey $1 or $9, or they can be combined to convey $19, $91, $19.19, and so on. This numbering system is called the decimal system. You use this system when you dial the phone, look up pages in the index of a book, or address a letter to a specific street address.

The familiar decimal system is complicated. To master the system in grade school, you had to memorize numerous tables. For example, to add 2 + 2, you do not calculate, you recall the answer 4 from memory. To multiply 3 × 2, you recall the answer 6 from memory. If you never learned the tables or forgot them, you would find it hard or even impossible to calculate with the decimal system.

Computers and other digital equipment use a simpler numbering system, the binary system. The binary system uses only two numbers, 0 and 1, to store, process, and display all digits. As the table "Decimal and Binary Equivalents" shows, any number can be conveyed with these two digits.

Binary numbers are used in computers because their two components, the 0 and 1, can be stored, processed, and communicated by devices that have two states. For example:

- If a device can be turned on and off, on can represent 1 and off 0.
- If a device can emit high or low voltage, the high voltage can represent 1 and the low voltage 0.

DECIMAL AND BINARY EQUIVALENTS

Decimal Number	Binary Equivalent
0	0
1	1
2	10
3	11
4	100
5	101
6	110
7	111
8	1000
9	1001
10	1010
11	1011

- If magnetic particles can be aligned on a surface so that they point in opposite directions, one direction can represent 1 and the other 0.
- If dots on a display screen can be either illuminated or dark, 1 can tell the screen to illuminate a dot and 0 to leave it dark.
- If a printer can print black spots onto a white sheet of paper, 1 can tell the printer to print a black dot and 0 to leave it white.

All these techniques are used in microcomputer systems to store, process, and communicate data. To take it one step further, you can convey information with these two digits if you have an agreed-on code. Let's now see how various devices and codes can be used to convey information.

Paul Revere's Ride—The First Digital Revolution?

You may have heard or read Longfellow's poem *Paul Revere's Ride*. Here are a few stanzas of the poem.

> *Listen, my children, and you shall hear*
> *Of the midnight ride of Paul Revere,*
> *On the eighteenth of April, in Seventy-five;*
> *Hardly a man is now alive*
> *Who remembers that famous day and year.*
>
> *He said to his friend, "If the British march*
> *By land or sea from the town tonight,*
> *Hang a lantern aloft in the belfry arch*
> *Of the North Church as a signal light,—*
> *One, if by land, and two, if by sea;*
> *And I on the opposite shore will be,*
> *Ready to ride and spread the alarm*
> *Through every Middlesex village and farm,*
> *For the country folk to be up and to arm."*

"One, if by land, and two, if by sea" is a digital message. When America was a colony of England, Paul Revere was assigned the responsibility of notifying the Minutemen who lived in the countryside if the British left Boston to attack them. He and his friend Robert Newman, the sexton of Old North Church, decided that Revere would wait on the other side of the harbor so that he had a head start should the British troops begin to move. Newman would remain in Boston to watch for any troop movements. Newman would light one lantern in the belfry of Old North Church if the British were leaving Boston by land and two lanterns if they were going by sea. This simple digital signal sent Paul Revere on his famous ride that resulted in "the shot heard round the world" at the bridge in Concord.

The Telegraph—The First Digital Code

Lanterns have their limits when it comes to sending information. It is hard to spell out messages. For example, if the British had been able to take an unexpected route, Paul Revere's prearranged code would not have been able to convey the message. This problem was solved by Samuel Morse's invention of the telegraph in the late 1830s.

The Lanterns in the Belfry
Two lanterns were used to signal Paul Revere which way the British were heading.

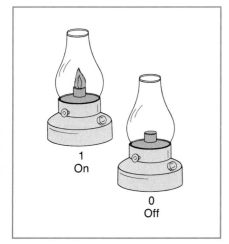

1
On

0
Off

When one lamp was on (1) and the other was off (0), it meant the British were moving by land.

1
On

1
On

When both lamps were on (1), it meant the British were moving by sea.

The First Digital Code
The telegraph was used to send dots and dashes down a wire to a recipient at the other end of the line.
Bettmann Archive, Inc.

A Silicon Chip
In computers, hundreds of "chips" are etched together onto a large silicon wafer (top). Each chip contains millions of transistors and is cut from the wafer and mounted on a larger board to which wires can be connected (bottom). These chips are the reason modern computers are so small.
Courtesy Hewlett Packard

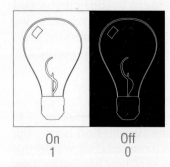

On   Off
1   0

A Bit
A bit is like a light bulb–it is either on to indicate 1 or off to indicate 0.

To send a telegraph message, you tap on a key to transmit pulses of electricity down a wire to a distant listener. At the listener's end, a device called a sounder clicks when each pulse arrives. Like the lanterns in the belfry, this is a digital process. However, random clicks do not convey information, so Morse developed a code based on the pauses between the clicks, using a short pause and a long pause. When printed, these were represented as dots and dashes. An experimental telegraph line was constructed between Baltimore and Washington, and on May 24, 1844, a series of long and short pauses between clicks sent the historic message "What hath God wrought" down this first telegraph line.

The Digital Computer
Like these early message systems, computers need a device that can send, process, or store information and a code to give the information meaning. Instead of lanterns or a key to send electrical pulses down a wire, a computer uses transistors. Like lanterns, transistors have only two possible states: on and off. When thousands of transistors are packed together, it is called an integrated circuit, or silicon chip. These chips store and process large amounts of information. Instead of using a code of long and short pauses, as Morse did, a microcomputer uses the transistor's on and off states. The code is based on *bits* and groups of bits called *bytes*.

Bits
The smallest unit stored or processed in a computer is the *bit*, a contraction of the more descriptive phrase **bi**nary dig**it**. In the computer, on (or 1) is represented by a high voltage, and off (or 0) is represented by a low voltage. On a magnetic disk, the same information is stored by changing the direction in which magnetized particles on the disk's surface are aligned.

To visualize a bit, imagine a light bulb. When the light bulb is on, it represents the number 1. When it is off, it represents the number 0. You could send a message to a nearby recipient by turning the bulb on and off, but to send even a short message would take a long time.

Bytes
Since bits are small units and can convey only two possible states, they are organized into larger units to convey more information. This larger unit is a *byte*, and it contains 8 bits. Since each bit has two states and there are 8 bits in a byte, the total amount of information that can be conveyed is 2^8 (2 raised to the 8th power), or 256 possible combinations.

A Byte

To understand a byte, imagine using eight light bulbs instead of one. Each letter in the alphabet could be assigned a pattern of lights. For example, this pattern could represent the letter A.

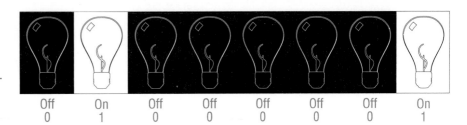

Off	On	Off	Off	Off	Off	Off	On
0	1	0	0	0	0	0	1

CHARACTERS AND THEIR ASCII CODES

Character	ASCII Code
A	0100 0001
a	0110 0001
B	0100 0010
b	0110 0010

To give meaning to each of these combinations, they must be assigned a code. The code can specify that each of them represents a letter, number, symbol, or command to the computer. For example, the number 0100 0001 can stand for the letter A.

Usually, you see these numbers converted to characters such as letters, numbers, and symbols displayed on the screen. To standardize the meaning of these number combinations, the computer industry uses several codes, including the **A**merican **S**tandard **C**ode for **I**nformation **I**nterchange, or ASCII (pronounced "as-key"), the code frequently used on microcomputers. The table "Characters and Their ASCII Codes" lists some typical characters and their ASCII codes.

FROM BYTES TO GIGABYTES

Power	Actual Bytes	Shorthand
2^0	1	1 byte
2^1	2	2 bytes
.	.	.
2^{10}	1,024	1KB (kilobyte)
2^{11}	2,048	2KB
2^{12}	4,096	4KB
.	.	.
2^{18}	262,144	256KB
2^{19}	524,288	512KB
2^{20}	1,048,576	1MB (megabyte)
2^{21}	2,097,152	2MB
2^{22}	4,194,304	4MB
.	.	.
2^{30}	1,073,741,824	1GB (gigabyte)

Shorthand

Most references to a computer's storage and processing capacity use the byte as the basic unit of measurement. The number of bytes is usually given in shorthand. For example, you'll see advertisements that say a computer's memory is 640,000 bytes, or 640KB. The KB (for kilobyte) indicates a magnitude of 1,000. As memory increases, the KB is replaced by an MB (for megabyte), which indicates a magnitude of 1,000,000. For example, you can say the computer's memory is 1,000,000 bytes, 1,000KB, or 1MB. As computer capacity expands, you'll begin to encounter the next levels of magnitude: the gigabyte (1 billion bytes) and the terabyte (1 trillion bytes).

When we refer to bytes in this way, we round the numbers to make them easier to remember. Bytes are calculated by raising the number 2 to various powers. The number 2 is used because digital devices have two states—on and off. The number 2 raised to the 10th power is 1,024. This is usually rounded off to 1,000 (or 1KB). The table "From Bytes to Gigabytes" shows the number 2 raised to some of the powers between 0 and 30, the actual bytes that result, and how these bytes are expressed in shorthand as kilobytes, megabytes, or gigabytes.

▶ EXERCISE

BYTES, KILOBYTES, AND MEGABYTES

Bytes	Kilobytes	Megabytes
1,024	_____	_____
524,288	_____	_____
1,048,576	_____	_____
2,097,152	_____	_____
16,777,216	_____	_____

EXERCISE 1

CONVERTING BYTES, KILOBYTES, AND MEGABYTES

Memory and other devices are frequently described in terms of bytes, kilobytes, and megabytes. In the table "Bytes, Kilobytes, and Megabytes," bytes are listed in the first column. In the next two columns, indicate the number of bytes in kilobytes and then in megabytes. Round off where necessary.

The Anatomy of a Microcomputer

Supercomputers
Supercomputers are powerful computers used to solve scientific problems and manipulate large graphic files.
Courtesy of Cray Research Inc.

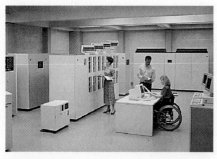

Mainframe Computers
The mainframe computer is often the corporate workhorse, occupying an entire room all by itself and maintained and operated by a highly trained staff of specialists.
Courtesy of IBM Corporation

Minicomputers
Minicomputers are smaller than mainframes and are normally used for departmental computing.
Courtesy of IBM Corporation

After completing this topic, you will be able to:
- Describe the function of the central processing unit (CPU)
- Explain how peripheral equipment such as a printer is attached to the computer
- Describe how "boards" can be plugged into expansion slots in the computer to expand its capabilities and improve its performance
- List things to do and to avoid doing with your computer

Computers come in many designs, but one way to classify them is according to their size, power, and portability.

- Supercomputers are the most powerful computers available. They are used for many scientific and technical applications, including weather forecasting and automotive design. They are also used to generate the extremely realistic graphics seen in many movie special effects.
- Mainframe computers are room-sized computers operated by a special staff. They are normally used for centralized business functions such as accounting and inventory control.
- Minicomputers are less powerful than mainframe computers and are anywhere from refrigerator size to desktop size. They are frequently used by small companies or by departments within large corporations.

More recently, advances in technology allowed for the development of smaller, more personal computers.

- Desktop computers, those used by individuals, are designed to be permanently positioned on a desk. Portable computers (also called *transportables*) are smaller than desktop computers so that they can be carried, but you wouldn't want to carry one with you on a subway or a long walk through an airport terminal.
- Laptop computers can be carried like a small attaché case or packed in a suitcase. They are designed so that they can run on rechargeable battery packs. Notebook computers are like laptops but even smaller, so they can be easily carried in a briefcase. In that sense, they are almost as convenient as a pocket calculator. However, they are working computers that can run programs and exchange information with other, larger computers.
- Handheld, or palm-top, computers have very small keyboards, so they cannot be easily used for word processing or other applications that require you to enter a lot of data. However, their small size makes them useful in many special applications. For example, salespeople use them to record customers' inventories,

and others use them to make calculations and maintain appointment schedules and phone numbers and addresses.

The Central Processing Unit

The heart of a computer is the central processing unit (CPU). In microcomputers, the CPU is a microprocessor—the device that made microcomputers possible in the first place. Though small, a microprocessor is extremely powerful; it (along with its operating system software) performs three key functions:

- It coordinates all the computer's activities. For example, it retrieves files from the disk, interprets data and commands entered from the keyboard, and sends data to a printer.
- It performs arithmetic calculations like addition and subtraction. For example, if you enter a list of numbers in a spreadsheet and ask for the total, the microprocessor performs the addition.
- It performs logical operations using equal to, greater than, and less than comparisons. For example, it can determine if your grades are higher or lower than those of other students in the same course, and it can print a list ranking everyone in descending order of the grades they received.

The speed and power of a computer are largely determined by the microprocessor that is used for its CPU. New microprocessors are periodically introduced as advances in technology allow them to be improved, and quite a number of versions are in widespread use. For example, the earliest IBM PCs used the Intel 8088 or 8086 chip. The IBM AT computers introduced next used the Intel 80286 (called the 286). Today, the most widely used chip in IBM and compatible computers is the Intel 80386 (called the 386), but it is being replaced on newer computer models by the Intel i486 (called the 486), and widespread use of the i586 is in the near future.

The most recent microprocessors are available in at least two versions and sometimes three. The full-featured versions are referred to by their numbers alone, for example, 386 and 486, or with the suffix *dx*, for example, 386dx and 486dx. Slightly less powerful but also less expensive versions use the suffix *sx*, for example, 386sx and 486sx. Finally, there is a version called the 486dx2 that is faster than a 486sx but slightly slower than a 486dx. The 2 following the dx indicates that the chip runs twice as fast internally as it does when it communicates with other parts of the computer.

The Microprocessor
The microprocessor is an extremely small but powerful device that is used as the central processing unit (CPU) in the microcomputer.
Courtesy of IBM Corporation

Clock Rates
The clock rate of a computer determines how fast it runs and affects how powerful it is.

IBM MICROPROCESSOR CHIPS

Microprocessor	Speed (MHz)	Date
8086 or 8088	4.7	1981
80286	8-12	1982
80386dx	25	1988
80386sx	16	1988
80386dx	33	1989
i486dx	25	1989
80386sx	20	1989
i486dx	33	1990
i486sx	20	1991
i486dx	50	1991
i486dx2	50	1992
i486dx2	66	1992

The version of the microprocessor is not the only consideration when you are choosing a computer. Another important variable is the *clock rate*, which is specified in megahertz (millions of cycles per second, or MHz). The clock rate indicates the speed at which the chip processes data. Like a caller at a square dance, it sets the pace for all activity. The higher the clock rate, the faster the computer. For example, a 33 megahertz 386 is faster than a 20 megahertz 386.

For most applications in a work environment where speed is essential, computers with 386sx chips are now becoming the minimum requirement.

The table "IBM Microprocessor Chips" lists the Intel microprocessor chips used in various IBM and compatible computers and the date they were first shipped to manufacturers.

Memory

For the computer's CPU to process data, it must have access to the data and instructions, called programs. The data and programs are normally stored in the computer's internal memory when they are being used. There are two types of internal memory—read-only memory (ROM) and random-access memory (RAM).

Read-Only Memory (ROM)

Read-only memory (ROM) is static, unchanging memory. Your computer can read data stored in ROM, but you cannot enter data into ROM or change the data already there. The data in ROM are permanently recorded on memory chips by the computer's manufacturer. Neither turning the computer off nor electrical failure affects it; the data will still be there when you resume. ROM is generally used to store programs and instructions that the computer frequently needs. For example, it contains the instructions your computer follows to start up when you first turn it on.

Random-Access Memory (RAM)

Random-access memory (RAM) is also called main, primary, or user memory. When you load a program into the computer or create a document with an application program, the program you load and the data you enter from the keyboard are temporarily stored in RAM. Usually, if you turn off the computer, any programs or data stored in this memory are lost; thus RAM is said to be volatile memory.

The term *random* comes from the way the data in memory can be located, or accessed, by the computer. One way to understand random access is to think of the differences between a tape player and a compact disc player. If you want to play the third song on a tape, you must advance the tape past the first two songs. This is called sequential access because you must access each song in sequence. On a compact disc player, you can advance directly to the track where the third song begins without having to play the first two songs. This is called random access because you can access songs in any order.

Ports

A computer system's external components, or peripherals, may include a printer, display screen, modem, keyboard, and mouse. You connect these peripherals to the computer with cables that plug into sockets mounted on the computer's cabinet. These sockets are called ports because, like seaports where ships enter and leave a country and airports where airplanes enter and leave a city, they are where signals carrying information enter and leave the computer. Some ports are dedicated to specific devices such as the keyboard, but there are two versatile ports—serial ports and parallel ports.

Memory

The Scrabble brand crossword game is like a computer's memory. The instruction book is like ROM—you can read it, but you cannot change it. The game board is like RAM—you can add, delete, or move data around on it.

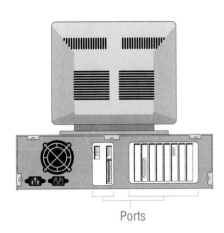

Ports

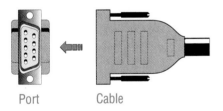

Port   Cable

Ports

Ports are where data enter and leave the computer. Ports are mounted on the back of the computer. You plug cables into ports to connect peripherals such as printers and mice.

Serial Ports

A serial port is like a single-lane tunnel. Information fed to it has to squeeze through the port a single bit at a time.

Serial Ports

Serial ports (sometimes called RS-232-C ports) are where you attach mice, modems (devices used to communicate with other computers), and some types of printers. When data are sent out of a serial port, they are sent 1 bit at a time. Since the data are processed inside the computer 8, 16, or even 32 bits at a time, a serial port is like a narrowing on a highway where it enters a narrow tunnel. Data slows down, just as the highway traffic does, so that they can funnel out of the computer in single file.

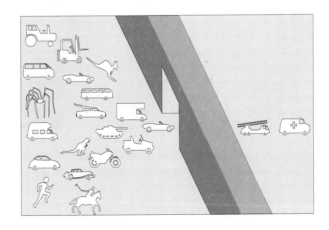

Parallel Ports

Parallel ports (sometimes called Centronics interfaces) carry data 8 bits at a time on parallel paths. Because they can transmit data 8 bits, or 1 byte, at a time, they are a faster way for the computer to communicate with input and output devices. There is less narrowing than on a serial port, so traffic moves faster. Parallel ports are usually used to plug in certain types of printers.

Parallel Ports
A parallel port is like a tunnel with almost the same number of lanes as the highway that feeds it. Information flows through faster since there is little or no constriction.

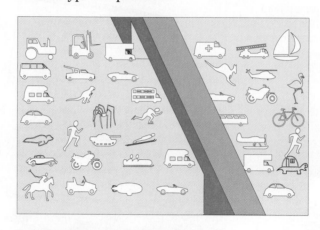

Expansion Slots and Boards

Many users like to customize or update their computers to better serve their needs. To make this possible, most computers have expansion slots inside the cabinet into which you can plug boards (also called *cards* and *adapters* and sometimes prefaced with *add-on*, *add-in*, or *expansion*). Boards plugged into these slots perform just as if they were built into the computer. Boards can serve any one of many functions. For example, boards can be added to expand the computer's memory, allow the computer to display colors or graphics, send and receive FAXes, or call up other computers. Still others connect peripherals or are the peripherals themselves. For example, you can plug in a board that controls a hard disk drive located elsewhere in the system, or you can plug in a board that contains the hard disk drive itself.

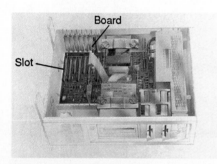

Expansion Slots and Boards
Expansion slots inside the computer allow you to plug in boards that expand the computer's capabilities.
Courtesy of IBM Corporation

Inside a Computer
If you were to remove the cover from a microcomputer, you would see a green circuit board (called the motherboard). All other elements are either mounted onto this board or connected to it. In this photograph, you can see the power supply (upper right) and a silver-colored floppy and black hard disk (bottom).
Courtesy of IBM Corporation

Caring for Your Computer

Computers are rugged and will provide good service with minimal maintenance if you treat them properly. Here are a few important dos and don'ts that will ensure you get the maximum life out of your equipment.

- **DO** turn down the screen intensity or use a screen-saving program if you will not be working on the computer for a while so that an image is not burned into the display screen's phosphor surface.
- **DO** use a surge protector between the computer and the wall outlet to protect the computer from any surges of electricity that might come down the power line. Surges occur when the power company restores service after it has been lost or when a nearby line is struck by lightning. A surge temporarily increases the current in the line, much as a wave of water is created when you suddenly remove a dam from a river. This surge of current can damage a computer.
- **DON'T** use it during lightning storms. If fact, to be completely safe, unplug it when there is lightning.
- **DON'T** get it wet.
- **DON'T** drop it.
- **DON'T** smoke around it.
- **DON'T** leave it where it is exposed to direct sunlight.
- **DON'T** turn it off more often than necessary. Computers, like other electronic equipment, are harmed more by the surge of power that runs through them when you first turn them on than they are by being left on all the time. Some users never turn their computers off; others turn them off only at the end of the day or on weekends.
- **DON'T** use an ultrasonic humidifier without a mineral filter near the computer. These units break the water and minerals into particles that are then distributed throughout the room. When the particles land on a computer, the water evaporates, leaving behind a powder that can damage sensitive equipment.

MAINFRAMES AND MICROS

As late as 1977, nearly 100% of the world's computer power was commanded by mainframe and other large computers with dumb terminals attached. (A dumb terminal is a screen and keyboard that can send and receive data to and from a computer, but which isn't a computer itself.) By 1987, less than 1% of the world's computer power was commanded by large computers. U.S. companies controlled some two-thirds of a global computer market of 90 million personal computers, more than half of them in the U.S.*
*From "The Drexel Era," *The Wall Street Journal*, February 16, 1990, p. A12.

THE DEVELOPMENT OF THE COMPUTER

The first electronic digital computer built in the United States, ENIAC, was unveiled at the University of Pennsylvania in 1946. It weighed 30 tons, filled the space of a two-car garage, and contained 18,000 vacuum tubes, which failed on average at the rate of one every seven minutes. It cost half a million dollars at 1946 prices.
Today, the same amount of computing power is contained in a pea-sized silicon chip. Almost any home computer costing as little as $100 can outperform ENIAC. Put another way, if the automobile and airplane businesses had developed like the computer business, a Rolls Royce would cost $2.75 and run for 3 million miles on one gallon of gas. And a Boeing 767 would cost just $500 and circle the globe in twenty minutes on five gallons of gas.*
*Tom Forester, ed., *The Information Technology Revolution* (Cambridge, Mass.: MIT Press, 1985).

EXERCISE 1

DESCRIBING COMPUTERS IN THE LAB

List and describe in the table "Computers in the Lab" one or more of the computers in your lab. Because some of the information is not noted on the computer, you may have to ask your instructor or refer to the computer's manual.

A. Who is the manufacturer of each computer? Typical manufacturers are IBM and Compaq. If the computer is not one of these brands, does it act as if it were; for example, is it compatible with IBM's products?

B. What models are the computers? For example, they might be IBM PCs, XTs, ATs, or PS/2s.

C. How much random-access memory (RAM) does each computer have?

D. What kind of microprocessor (chip) does each use?

E. How many expansion slots does each have?

COMPUTERS IN THE LAB

Manufacturer/ID	Model	RAM	Chip	Number of Slots
_____	_____	_____	_____	_____
_____	_____	_____	_____	_____
_____	_____	_____	_____	_____
_____	_____	_____	_____	_____
_____	_____	_____	_____	_____

EXERCISE 2

IDENTIFYING YOUR COMPUTER'S PORTS

Sketch the back of one of the computers in the lab, and then label the ports to which the peripherals are attached. They are probably not labeled on the computer, so you may have to ask your instructor or lab assistant. Try to identify the following ports, and then list what is attached to them:

A. Parallel port
B. Serial port
C. Keyboard port
D. Mouse port

Input and Output Devices

After completing this topic, you will be able to:
- Describe the keys on the computer's keyboard
- Describe how a mouse works
- Explain how scanners can input text and graphics
- Explain the differences between character and graphics display modes
- Explain how different types of printers form images on paper
- List and describe common printer features and controls

For a computer to be useful, you must be able to get information into or out of it. It is the input and output devices that perform this crucial role. The most common input device is the keyboard. The most common output devices are the display screen and printer.

The Keyboard
Keyboards vary in design and layout from computer to computer, but all have essentially the same types of keys. For example, two types of keyboards are used with most IBM or compatible computers—the original IBM PC keyboard and the enhanced keyboard introduced with the IBM AT. The main differences between the older and newer keyboards are the locations of the function keys and the directional arrow keys.

When you press keys on a keyboard, you should do so smoothly and quickly, just as if you were typing on a typewriter. Many keys have an autorepeat feature. If you hold one of these keys down, it will continue entering the key's character or repeating its function until you release it. Although this feature is occasionally useful, it can cause problems when you are first learning because strange things may happen when you hold a key down too long.

Keyboard Lights
Many keyboards have lights that indicate the status of the (CapsLock), (NumLock), and (ScrlLock) keys. Each of these keys toggles like a wall switch. If it is not engaged when you press it, it becomes engaged. If it is engaged when you press it, it becomes disengaged. When any of these keys are engaged, the corresponding keyboard indicator light will be lit.

Cursor Movement Keys
Cursor movement keys move the cursor around the screen. You use the cursor to point to where you want to enter or edit data on the screen. Because program designers can change their functions, the keys used to move the cursor vary from program to program. However, the directional arrow keys move the cursor one line or character at a time

The Cursor
The cursor is a one-character-wide highlight that you move about the screen to enter, edit, and format text. Its shape can vary, but it is usually an underline or rectangle that highlights a single character.

in the direction of the arrow. On most programs, the PgUp and PgDn keys move the cursor a screen or page at a time.

Keyboards

These figures show the regular and enhanced keyboards. They are similar except for the location of the function keys and an extra set of cursor movemenet keys on the enhanced keyboard.

The Regular Keyboard

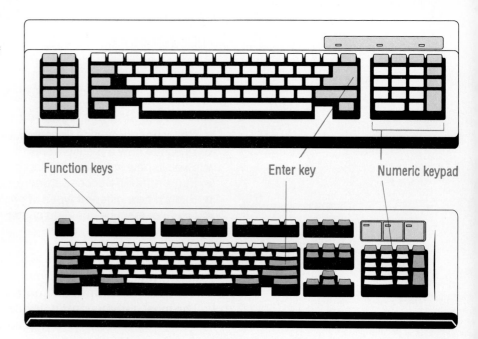

Function keys   Enter key   Numeric keypad

The Enhanced Keyboard

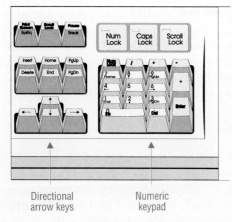

Directional arrow keys   Numeric keypad

Directional Arrow Keys

All computers have directional arrow keys on the numeric keypad that work only when NumLock is not engaged. Enhanced keyboards have a separate set of directional arrow keys that work whether NumLock is engaged or not.

Entering and Editing Keys

Most of the keys on a keyboard are used to enter or edit data. The alphabetic keys are arranged just as they are on a typewriter. When you press these keys, you enter lowercase letters. If you hold down the ⇧ Shift key when you press them, or if you engage the CapsLock key, you enter uppercase (capital) letters. If you engage CapsLock and then hold down ⇧ Shift while typing, you enter lowercase letters.

If you are an experienced typist and are used to typing a lowercase L for 1 or an uppercase O for 0 (zero), do not do this on your computer. The computer treats numbers and letters differently, and you will run into difficulties by disregarding this distinction.

Numeric keys are located above the alphabetic keys and are labeled with both numbers and symbols. When you press these keys, you enter either the indicated numbers or, if you hold down ⇧ Shift, the indicated symbols. On many computers, you can also enter numbers using the numeric keypad at the right end of the keyboard. Since some of the keys on the numeric keypad also move the cursor, you must press NumLock to switch back and forth between entering numbers and moving the cursor. When NumLock is engaged, the keys enter numbers. When it is not engaged, they move the cursor.

The Spacebar moves the cursor one character to the right and enters a space. If there is a character to the right of the cursor, it may be pushed to the right or replaced by a blank space depending on how the program is set up.

The ← Bksp key backs the cursor up and usually deletes characters as it does so. This lets you quickly back over and delete characters when you discover a mistake while entering text.

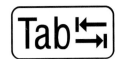

Tab and Backtab
The tab and backtab functions are both on the same key. It acts as backtab when you hold down ⇧ Shift.

The Shift Key
The ⇧ Shift key has an up arrow on it to indicate that it shifts to uppercase letters when held down.

The Tab⇆ key moves the cursor to the next tab stop, and the ⇧ Shift - Tab⇆ key moves it back to the previous tab stop.

Command Keys
Many keys on the keyboard are used to execute commands rather than to enter or edit data. Although the function of many keys varies from program to program, the following functions usually apply:

The Enter↵ key (also called the **Return** key) is often pressed as the final keystroke of an operation. For example, when you type a command or highlight one on a menu, you have to press Enter↵ to send the command to the CPU.

The Esc (Escape) key is often (but by no means always) used to cancel a command in progress.

Function keys (designated F1, F2, F3, and so on) perform functions assigned to them by the programmer. For example, on a word processing program, function keys are often assigned to select, copy, move, or delete text. On some keyboards, the function keys are grouped at the left side of the keyboard. On other computers, they are the top row of keys.

Many keys are assigned more than one function. For instance, pressing the right directional arrow key may move the cursor one column or character at a time, but pressing the same key while holding down the Ctrl (Control) key may move the cursor several columns or characters at a time. Pressing the letter B enters the letter alone, but pressing B while holding down the Alt (Alternate) key might enter a code that tells the printer to begin boldfacing text. Ctrl and Alt do not send characters to the computer; they change what is sent when you press other keys. Using combinations of keys in this way lets software designers assign many more functions to the keyboard than there are keys. This is much like the standard typewriter, which uses **Shift** to enter fifty-two characters (twenty-six uppercase and twenty-six lowercase letters) with only twenty-six keys.

When you use these modifier keys, you hold them down first and then press the other key. The sequence in which you press the keys is important, so follow these procedures:

1. Hold down the Alt, ⇧ Shift, or Ctrl key. These keys do not repeat or send commands to the computer, so you can hold them down as long as you want.
2. Press the function key just as if you were typing a character, then release both keys. If you hold the second key down, the command may repeat over and over until you release it, and this can create problems.

Mice
Many programs have added support for a mouse. As you move the mouse around on a flat, smooth surface, it moves a mouse pointer on the screen so that you can point to items. You can use a mouse for several procedures, including the following:

■ Making menu choices from pull-down menus
■ Moving the cursor through a document or other file
■ Selecting (blocking) data so that they can be copied, moved, deleted, or formatted

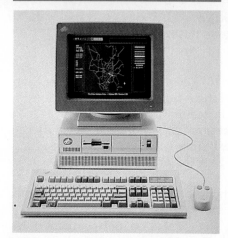

A Mouse
Mice are used to point to and then click on commands to execute them or to drag items about on the screen.
Courtesy of IBM Corporation

When you use a mouse for the first time, you will experience some frustration. It seems hard to point to just the right place and to click or hold the button at the right time. Don't let these frustrations get you down; everyone experiences them. In a few days, you'll wonder how you ever got along without a mouse. However, once you have mastered it, you have to decide when to put it down. Many operations can be performed faster from the keyboard. Users who continually switch back and forth between the keyboard and a mouse actually work slower than those who think through the fastest approach to a task.

When you use a mouse, you roll it across the surface of the desk. This motion tells the mouse which way to move the mouse pointer on the screen. To make the mouse pointer move in a predictable direction, it is important that you hold the mouse so that it is oriented parallel to the center line of the screen. This way, when you move the mouse up, down, or sideways, the mouse pointer moves in the expected direction. If you hold the mouse at an angle, your hand motion and the motion of the mouse pointer will not be coordinated.

When you use a mouse, here are some basic terms to remember:

- The *mouse pointer* refers to the arrow or other symbol on the screen that moves when you move the mouse.
- *Point* means to position the mouse pointer over or on some items on the screen.
- *Clicking* refers to pressing one of the buttons on the mouse.
- *Double clicking* refers to pressing one of the buttons on the mouse twice in rapid succession.
- *Drag* means to hold down one of the mouse buttons while you move the mouse. You do this frequently when you want to highlight a block of text so that you can format it. In other situations, this action drags the highlighted item to a new position on the screen.

Scanners

You do not have to type everything into a computer. Scanners allow you to enter text and graphics from hardcopy such as printed or typed documents, photographs, or line drawings. You have seen scanners at work whenever you visit the supermarket. At the checkout counter, a clerk runs a handheld wand over a product or passes the product over a slot in the counter. These devices read the bar code on the product and display its price on the register. They also record the sale and make adjustments in inventory so that the store knows when to reorder. In most situations, however, scanners are used to scan text and graphics into the computer.

Text Scanners
When you type text into a computer and then print it out on a printer, you are actually converting the text from a digital form (the form used by the computer) to a printed form. Until recently, it was not easy to go the other way—to convert printed copy into an electronic form that could be processed by a computer. To make this conversion more efficient, scanners and optical character recognition (OCR) software have been developed to automate the process.

The scanner reads the pattern of dark characters against a light background, and the software converts each character to its digital ASCII number. This ASCII number is then stored in the computer's

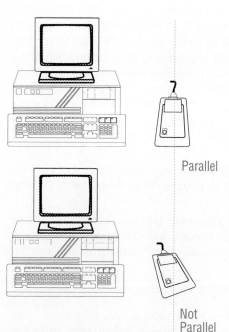

Parallel

Not Parallel

Holding and Dragging a Mouse
Hold the mouse parallel to the center line of the screen and when you move it, the mouse pointer on the screen will move in a predictable direction.

CRT Displays
CRT displays create a sharp and readable image with a TV-like tube.
Courtesy of IBM Corporation

Flat Panel Displays
Flat panel displays are very thin, so they are used mostly in laptop and notebook computers.
Courtesy of IBM Corporation

memory or on a disk. Because the text is converted into its ASCII numbers, it can be stored, displayed, printed, and otherwise manipulated just as if it had been entered into the computer with the keyboard.

Graphics Scanners
To scan graphic images such as photographs, line drawings, charts, and maps into the computer, you use a scanner and graphics scanning software. The scanner works by breaking the image up into small spots, called pixels (for picture elements). It then assigns a numeric value to each pixel and stores it in memory or on the disk. The image can then be incorporated into a word-processed or desktop published document or manipulated with a program designed to work with images of this kind.

Display Screens

Many microcomputer display screens (also called monitors) are based on a cathode ray tube (CRT) like the one used in television sets. Others, such as those used in laptop and notebook computers, use light-emitting diodes (LEDs) or liquid crystal displays (LCDs), among other technologies, to create the image.

When you load a program, the display that you see on the screen is either a character display or a graphics display. These two types of screen displays are referred to as character mode and graphics mode. Which mode you see depends both on the system you are using and the program you are running. Most computer systems today are capable of displaying graphics, but many programs do not yet take advantage of this feature; they run in character mode.

Character Mode
When microcomputers were first developed, most systems displayed just letters, numbers, and a very limited set of other special characters (such as ∎). Altogether, 256 characters, called the character set, could be displayed and nothing else. Because of this limitation to a fixed set of characters, this is called character mode.

Character mode has the advantage of requiring little memory and operating very fast. Unfortunately, it also has several disadvantages. Since it can display only the characters in the computer's character set, it can display only simple graphics such as lines and boxes. Moreover, characters must occupy a fixed position on the screen and are all the same size. This prevents you from seeing different typefaces and type sizes until you make a printout. Finally, character mode cannot display photographs or line drawings.

Character Mode

Character mode displays only a limited number of characters and simple graphics. Here, a typical character mode program is shown.

```
TOPIC 1
Microcomputers

Computers come in many designs but one way to classify them is according to thei
power, and portability. First there were the large computers. More recently, adv
technology allowed for the development of smaller, more personal computers.
                                                    ┌FIG 1────────────────
■  Desktop computers, those used by individ-
   uals, are designed to be permanently
   positioned on a desk.
■  Portable computers (also called transport-
   ables) are smaller than desktop computers
   so that they can be carried, but you woul-
   dn't want to carry one with you on a sub-
   way or a long walk through an airport
   terminal.
■  Laptop computers can be carried like a
   small attache case or packed in a suitcase.
   They are designed so that they can run on
   rechargeable battery packs.
■  Notebook computers are like laptops but
   even smaller so they can be easily carried
   in a briefcase. In that sense, they are
H:\COMPUTE.WP5                              Doc 1 Pg 1 Ln 1" Pos 1"
```

Graphics Mode

In graphics mode, the screen is divided into a grid of picture elements, or pixels. When an image is displayed on the screen, some of the pixels are illuminated, and some are left dark. On a color monitor, the colors of each pixel can also be set. The patterns of illuminated or colored pixels form characters and other images on the screen. This flexibility allows text and illustrations to be displayed on the screen.

Graphics Mode

Graphics mode can display any character and any graphic because each is created from a pattern of small dots, called pixels. Since these dots can be arranged in any pattern, any image can be displayed. Here, the same document as shown in the figure "Character Mode" is displayed in graphics mode.

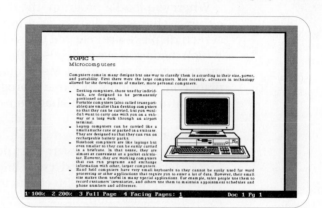

The resolution (sharpness) of a graphics display is determined by the number of pixels the screen is divided into. The resolution is indicated by the number of pixels displayed horizontally on the screen by the number displayed vertically. For example, a resolution of 320 by 200 pixels indicates the screen has 320 pixels horizontally and 200 vertically.

The resolution of a system is determined by which of the four most widely used standards, called display modes, it is using. In ascending order of sharpness, these modes are as follows:

■ Color graphics adapters (CGA) display 320-by-200 resolution.
■ Enhanced color graphics adapters (EGA) display 640-by-350 resolution.
■ Video graphics arrays (VGA) display 640-by-480 resolution.
■ Extended graphics arrays (XGA) display 1024-by-768 resolution. Many systems achieve this high resolution using a mode called Super VGA.

Screen Resolution

A high-resolution display screen is divided into more pixels than a low-resolution display is. The result is a sharper image because each character is formed from more dots.

High Resolution

Low Resolution

The graphics standard that your system uses is determined by the video display that is built into your computer or that was added by inserting a board into an expansion slot inside the computer. The monitor must exactly match the mode of the board, or it must be a multisync monitor that can display any of the popular modes. Multisync monitors are initially more expensive, but they allow you to upgrade to a higher resolution without buying a new monitor.

Although all the display modes can display colors, it is not essential that the monitor also do so. Since most printers cannot print colors, formatting a document for color is not usually important. There are several gray-scale monitors that are inexpensive (about one-third the cost of a color monitor of comparable quality) and give display quality similar to that of more expensive color monitors.

Graphics displays have several advantages. They can display different fonts, type sizes, and enhancements such as italics and proportional spacing. Also, both text and graphics can be displayed on the screen at the same time, which is especially important in desktop publishing applications. But there are also disadvantages; graphics displays require a lot of memory, and they operate more slowly than character displays.

WYSIWYG

The latest programs allow you to see on a graphics screen exactly what your document will look like before it is printed out. This is called WYSIWYG (pronounced "wizzy-wig"), or "What You See Is What You Get." WYSIWYG is now incorporated into high-end word processing and spreadsheet programs that have desktop publishing features. On programs that do not yet display a document for editing in WYSIWYG, this feature is offered as a document preview command that lets you see how the document will look when it is printed. Although you cannot edit a document in this preview mode, you can see where improvements might be made before you print it out. A true WYSIWYG display has the following features:

- Characters are displayed in the actual typeface, typestyle, and type size in which they will be printed.
- Paragraphs are displayed with the same line endings and line spacings with which they will be printed.
- Line drawings or photographs that are inserted into the document are displayed on the screen.
- Pages are displayed as they will print, including headers and footers, margins, and page numbers.
- Many programs have pull-down menus, icons, and scroll bars that make the programs easy to operate. These items make up what is known as a graphical user interface (GUI—pronounced "goo-ey").

Unfortunately, WYSIWYG displays are slow, even on the fastest computers. This is because much of the computer's processing power must be devoted to updating the screen display. For this reason, some programs allow you to switch back and forth between a WYSIWYG mode and a draft mode. In draft mode, graphics are not displayed, and some fonts are not displayed as they will appear when printed. This reduced display allows you to scroll through the document and make corrections much faster than when in WYSIWYG mode.

WYSIWYG

The latest programs designed for graphic displays feature WYSIWYG (What You See Is What You Get). This means the document on the screen looks almost exactly as it will look when printed. You might compare this figure with the "Character Mode" and "Graphics Mode" figures since all three show the same document.

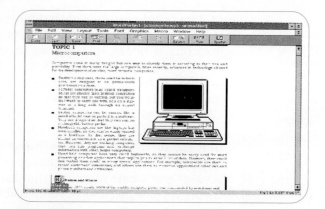

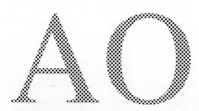

Printer Resolution

The quality of a printed character is determined by the spacing of the dots. This enlargement shows that the closer the dots are, the better the quality of the character.

Printed Graphics

Graphic images such as photographs are printed with dots. Here a partial enlargement shows how the image is formed from dots.

Printers

Most modern printers form characters using an array of dots. These printers are called raster printers, and there are several different types. The spacing of the dots affects the resolution, or quality, of the characters. For comparison, display monitors use about 50 to 100 dots per inch (dpi) to display text and images, dot-matrix printers 100 to 200, laser printers 300 to 600, and commercial typesetting machines 1,000 to 2,400.

Printers that print using an array of dots can also print graphics. By controlling the position dots are printed in, an illusion of brightness can be conveyed. The ability to convey brightness allows dot-matrix printers to print detailed line art and photographs.

Dot-Matrix Printers

One of the most common printers is called a dot-matrix printer. This printer uses a printhead containing pins, or wires, arranged in a column to print characters. As the printhead passes across the paper, the computer tells it which pins are to be fired to form a particular character. As the pins are fired, they strike an inked ribbon against the paper. The number of pins and dots determines the character's resolution. Less-expensive printers usually use 9 pins to create characters. More-expensive printers have 24 pins in their printheads.

Laser Printers

Laser printers, the most desirable type of printer, are very fast, usually printing eight or more pages per minute.

The resolution of laser printers is greater than that of dot-matrix printers because of the higher number of dots and their greater density. Most laser printers can print 300 dpi, and printers with 400 and more dpi are available. Despite the great number of dots, laser printers are fast and quiet because the dots are not transferred to the paper by mechanical devices that strike a ribbon.

Printer Features

Even with the best printers, there are differences that affect their use. Two of the more significant are memory and fonts.

Memory

Unlike dot-matrix printers, where data are taken from the computer and then printed a line at a time, laser printers make up an entire page before printing it. The page is temporarily stored in the printer's

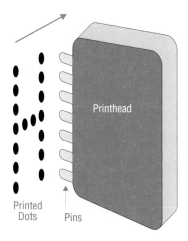

Dot-Matrix Printhead

Dot-matrix printers have a printhead that contains pins. These pins are "fired" against the inked ribbon to print characters on the page.

Laser Printers

Laser printers are now the printer of choice. They give superb results at a reasonable cost.
Courtesy of Hewlett Packard

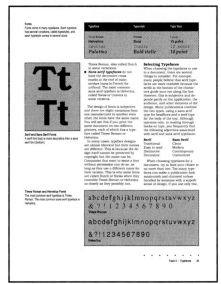

Laser-Printer Quality

Laser printers can print both text and graphics. The dots making up the image are so closely spaced that they look as if they were professionally printed.

memory while it is being processed and printed. If a page contains a graphics image, the memory required for it can be substantial. For example, it takes 1 megabyte to store a full-page black-and-white graphics image that is to be printed with a 300-dpi resolution. To fill the page, the printer has to address over 8 million dots (1 megabyte × 8 bits = 8 million bits). This is obviously a big chore.

If there isn't enough memory in the printer, only part of a page or image may be printed. As a rule of thumb, a laser printer should have at least 1 megabyte of memory, but if you are planning on printing large graphics or downloading fonts to the printer, you may need more.

Fonts

When you print a document, the way the characters look depends on the font used to print them. There are thousands of designs for type, each one different from the next. These different designs are referred to as fonts. All printers can print using fonts that are permanently stored in the printer's ROM (read-only memory). For some printers, other fonts are available in cartridges that are plugged into the printer. You can quickly access fonts stored in ROM and cartridge fonts, and they do not take up room on your computer's hard disk. Some printers, however, will accept downloadable fonts stored on the computer's hard disk. You can choose from the fonts on the disk and load them into the printer when you need them. This way, the printer has access to any fonts you want to use. Two types of fonts are available—bit-mapped and scalable.

- Bit-mapped fonts are made up of a series of dots and can be printed in only one size, the size they come in. If you need 8-, 10-, 12-, and 14-point versions, you must have a complete font in each size. Storage can be a problem as a result.
- Scalable fonts (also called *outline fonts*) are created on the fly while text is being printed by formulas stored in the computer or printer. These fonts allow a wide range of sizes while requiring very little space on the disk or in a printer's memory.

Using Printers

When you want to send a document to the printer, you first load the printer with paper and turn the printer on. The way you load paper depends on the type of printer and paper you are using. If you are using single sheets, you usually stack them in a paper tray or bin. If you are using fan-fold paper (also called continuous form paper), you feed it into the printer.

The settings you can make on the printer vary. However, many have some or all of the following switches:

- *On/Off* turns the power to the printer on and off. Knowing when to use this switch is important.
  - If you turn the printer off while it is operating, all data in its memory will be lost.
  - If you have canceled a print job and want to start over, turning the computer off and back on is a good way to ensure that text from the previous job does not remain in the printer's memory.
  - When you turn a dot-matrix printer on, it uses the line that the print element is resting on as the starting point when calculating top margins and page length. This is useful since you can

Courier
Times Roman (or Dutch)
Helvetica (or Swiss)

Printer Fonts

All printers have at least one built-in font. These are simply sets of characters that have different appearances. Here, the most common built-in fonts are shown.

turn off the printer, adjust your paper, and then turn it back on to set the top of the form.

■ *Off-Line/On-Line* connects the printer to and disconnects it from the computer. The printer must be on line to print documents, but it must be off line to use some of the other switches on the printer, such as Form Feed and Line Feed.

■ *Form Feed* (sometimes labeled FF) advances a sheet of paper out of the printer. If the printer has an automatic sheet feeder, it inserts a new sheet. For this switch to work, the printer must be off line.

■ *Line Feed* (sometimes labeled LF) advances paper in the printer by one line. This is useful when making fine adjustments to the paper's position in the printer. For this switch to work, the printer must be off line.

■ *Letter Quality/Draft Quality* switches a dot-matrix printer between its letter-quality mode (which is high quality but slower) and its draft-quality mode (which is lower quality but faster).

■ *Font* changes the default font so that the entire document is printed in that font unless you specified otherwise within the document being printed.

EJECTING PAPER

Many printers do not eject a printed sheet automatically. To manually advance a printed page out of your printer:

1. Press the printer's on-line switch to take it off line.
2. Press the printer's form-feed switch to advance or eject the page.
3. Press the printer's on-line switch to put it back on line.

> **E X E R C I S E S**

EXERCISE 1

IDENTIFYING KEYS ON THE KEYBOARD

Match the keyboard on your computer with one of those shown in the figures "Regular Keyboard" or "Enhanced Keyboard." Then identify the location of the following keys on the figure:

A. Alphabetic keys   F. Spacebar   J. Ctrl key

B. Numeric keys   G. ← Bksp key   K. Function keys

C. Numeric keypad   H. Esc key   L. NumLock key

D. Enter ↵ **(Return)**   I. ⇧ Shift keys   M. CapsLock key

E. Arrow keys

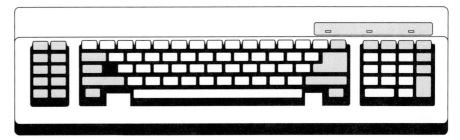

Regular Keyboard

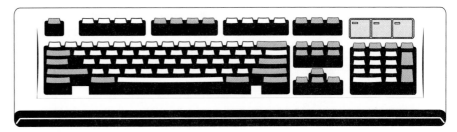

Enhanced Keyboard

EXERCISE 2

IDENTIFYING KEYBOARD INDICATORS

If one of the keyboards in the lab has indicator lights built into it, sketch the lights, and then label each of them as follows:

A. On/off indicator   C. CapsLock indicator

B. NumLock indicator   D. ScrlLock indicator

EXERCISE 3

IDENTIFYING THE PRINTER'S CONTROLS

Sketch and label the controls on one of the printers in the lab. Briefly describe the purpose of each control listed in the table "The Printer's Controls," and indicate the procedures you follow to use the control. For some of this information, you may have to ask your instructor or refer to the printer's manual.

THE PRINTER'S CONTROLS

Control	Description
On/off switch	_____
On line	_____
Form feed	_____
Line feed	_____
Fonts	_____
Other	_____

External Storage Devices

After completing this topic, you will be able to:
- List and describe the main features of floppy disks
- Explain how floppy and hard disk drives work
- Describe how data are stored on magnetic media
- Describe CD-ROM players and CD-ROM discs
- List and describe ways to protect and secure your data

When you work on a computer, the programs and files on which you work are stored internally in the computer's random-access memory (RAM). This memory is a limited resource, yet it must serve many uses. Not only do you load different application programs, you also create numerous files of your own work. The computer's memory is not large enough to store all the programs, documents, and other computer-generated files you work on. Moreover, most internal memory will lose its data when you turn the computer off.

External Storage

External storage is used to permanently store data and programs. Any data stored on an external storage device can be quickly moved into the computer's memory when needed.

RAM is temporary storage

Disks are permanent storage

For these reasons, external storage (also called auxiliary or secondary storage) is provided to store program files and data files that you are not using at the moment. Once data files are stored externally, you can reload them into the computer's internal memory without having to rekeyboard the data.

Computers usually use magnetic disks to store programs and files externally. Magnetic disks, and the devices used to store and retrieve data on them, fall into two major classes—floppy and hard disks and drives.

Floppy Disks

Floppy disks for microcomputers come in two sizes: 5¼ and 3½ inches. Each size works only with drives specifically designed to accept it. Though they vary in size, they have certain features in common:

Floppy Disk Characteristics

5¼-inch and 3½-inch disks have many features in common.

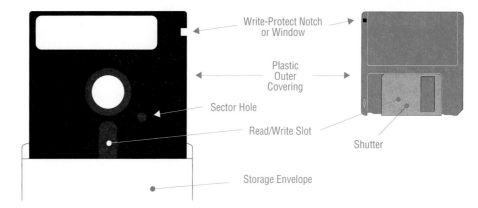

Write-Protect Notch or Window

Plastic Outer Covering

Sector Hole

Read/Write Slot

Shutter

Storage Envelope

1. A plastic outer covering protects the disk itself while allowing it to spin smoothly. A 5 -inch disk is protected by a flexible plastic jacket, whereas a 3 -inch disk is mounted in a rigid plastic housing. The jacket or housing is permanently sealed and contains lubricants and cleaning agents that prolong the life of the disk. A storage envelope protects 5 -inch disks from scratches, dust, and finger-prints. These envelopes are not used on the better-protected 3 -inch disks.

2. The read/write slot in the jacket is where the disk drive's read/write head contacts the surface of the disk. This read/write head stores data on (writes) and retrieves data from (reads) the surface of the disk as the disk spins inside the drive. On 3 -inch disks, the read/write slot is protected by a sliding metal cover called the shutter. When you insert the disk into the drive, this shutter is automatically pushed aside so that the read/write slot is exposed, and the drive can come in contact with the floppy disk within.

3. The write-protect notch or window allows you to write data to a disk when it is not write-protected and prevents you from writing to the disk when it is. (See the section "Write-Protecting Your Disks" on page 28.) A switch, or photoelectric circuit, inside the disk drive determines if the disk is write-protected. When it is, the switch disables the drive's ability to write data onto the disk.

If you were to remove the plastic jacket or housing of a floppy disk, you would find a round piece of plastic covered with a metallic oxide similar to the magnetic recording material used on audiotapes and videotapes. The round disk is sandwiched between two sheets of a soft, feltlike material, which is impregnated with a lubricant that protects the disk when it is spinning in the drive. The blank disk has three key features:

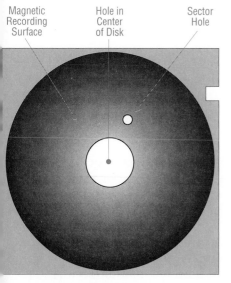

Magnetic Recording Surface

Hole in Center of Disk

Sector Hole

Inside a Floppy Disk

Inside a floppy disk there is a plastic disk, that has three key features.

1. The magnetic recording surface on which the data are stored occupies the outer portion of the disk. The density used to store data on this surface varies depending on your system. (For a detailed discussion of disk densities, see Topic 9.)

2. The large hole in the center of the disk is used by the drive to align and spin the disk. This hole is sometimes reinforced with a plastic hub and, on 3 -inch disks, is covered by a metal hub.

3. The sector hole, which is punched through the disk, is used by the computer to know where to store data to and retrieve data from the disk. A light is positioned in the drive so that it shines through the

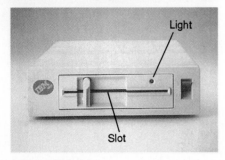

A Floppy Disk Drive
The floppy disk drive has two parts that you should be familiar with: the slot and the light. Here, they are shown on a standalone drive, but most disk drives are built into the computer.
Courtesy of IBM Corporation

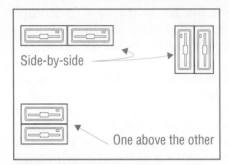

Inserting a Floppy Disk
The arrangement of floppy disk drives varies from computer to computer. If your floppy disk drives are side by side, drive A is usually the one on the left. If one drive is above the other, drive A is usually the one on the top.

Hard Disks
A hard disk uses rigid metal platters instead of a floppy disk to store data. These disks spin at over 3,000 revolutions per minute as data are written to the disk and read from it by a movable read/write head.
Courtesy of Seagate

sector hole on each revolution. When this happens, a photoelectric cell sees the light and signals the computer so that it can keep itself oriented to the disk's position, much as a ship can orient itself from a lighthouse beacon.

Floppy Disk Drives

The floppy disk drive is the device that the floppy disk is inserted into so that you can store data to and retrieve data from it. The floppy disk drive has two parts you should be familiar with: the slot and the light.

1. The slot is where you insert a floppy disk into the drive. The way you insert floppy disks depends on the type of system you are using.
   - To insert a 5¼-inch disk, open the door to the disk drive. Hold the disk with the label facing up to insert it into a horizontal drive or with the label facing to the left to insert it into a vertical drive. Point the oblong read/write slot toward the slot in the drive, and insert the disk into the slot. (On some systems, it clicks into place.) Never push hard because a 5¼-inch disk will buckle if it gets caught on an obstruction. Carefully jiggle the disk to make sure it is inserted all the way into the disk drive. Gently close the disk drive's door, or press the button that locks the disk into the drive. If you encounter any resistance, jiggle the disk, and then close the door or press the button again. To remove the disk, open the door and pull the disk out. On some drives, gently pushing it in and quickly releasing the pressure pops it out of the drive; on others, you have to press a button.
   - To insert a 3½-inch disk, hold it so that the arrow embossed on the case is facing up or to the left and pointing toward the drive's slot. Insert the disk gently into the drive, and then press until it clicks into place. To remove the disk, press the disk-eject button located near the drive's slot.
2. The light on the front of the drive goes on when the drive is operating. When the light is on, you should not open or close the door or eject a disk. Doing so can damage the disk or cause you to lose data. If you make a mistake and the drive spins when the door is open or without a disk inserted, do not close the door or insert a disk. In a few moments, a message will usually appear on the screen telling you the drive's door is open or no disk is in the drive. When the light goes out, close the door or insert a disk, and then follow the instructions displayed on the screen.

Hard Disk Drives

Hard disk drives (also called fixed disks) are now a necessity for serious computer users. Newer programs frequently require 2 or more megabytes of disk storage space. (One new word processing program requires 16 megabytes.) These programs cannot be run without a high-capacity hard disk drive.

Instead of a floppy disk, hard disk drives use rigid metal platters to store data. On such a platter, data can be stored more densely than on a floppy disk, and a drive can use more than one platter. As a result, hard disks with over 100 megabytes of storage capacity are now common. In addition, a hard disk drive spins at 3,600 rpm, about ten

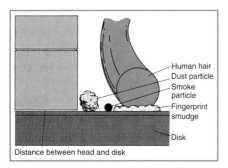

Hard Disk Tolerances
Hard disks have very small tolerances. When the read/write head is flying over the surface of the disk, the two are so close that smoke, a dust particle, a strand of hair, or even a fingerprint could cause the head to crash into the disk, causing damage to data.

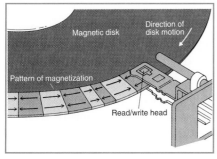

How Data Are Stored
Data are stored magnetically as the drive's read/write head moves over the disk. If the polarity of the magnetized area points in one direction, it is a 1; in the other, it is a 0.

CD-ROM
CD-ROM discs look like compact discs for music. These discs can store an enormous amount of information.
Courtesy of IBM

times faster than a floppy disk drive, allowing data to be stored and retrieved faster.

In a floppy disk drive, the read/write heads are in contact with the disk. In a hard disk drive, they fly over its surface on a cushion of air with a space smaller than a piece of dust separating the head from the rapidly spinning disk. To imagine the very small tolerances involved, picture an airplane flying at high speed ½ inch above the ground without making contact. With the high speeds and small spaces involved, even a dust particle can cause the read/write head to come in contact with the disk's surface, creating what is called a head crash. With the disk spinning at almost 60 mph, this can cause a lot of damage to the disk and the data stored on it.

To prevent small objects from damaging the drive or affecting its performance, hard disks are hermetically sealed in a case. When you use a hard disk drive, the read/write head is positioned on the disk where data are stored. Even slightly jarring your computer may damage your files. If you are going to move your computer, use the park program (usually found on a disk that comes with your computer) to park the read/write head. This program moves the read/write head to a section of the disk that has no data, thus preventing the head from damaging data on the disk should it move. You needn't do this on all systems because some have an autopark feature that parks the disk whenever you turn off the computer.

How Data Are Stored to and Retrieved from a Disk

Data are stored on a disk magnetically. If you have ever played with two magnets, you know that when held end to end, they attract each other. When one of them is then reversed, they repel each other. This is caused by a difference in polarity. Opposite polarities attract, and identical polarities repel. These two magnetic states are used to record data on a disk. As the disk spins, electrical signals in the read/write head change the polarity of magnetic particles on the disk's surface to record 0s and 1s. When you retrieve a file from the disk, the effect is reversed. The polarity of the disk immediately under the read/write head induces an electrical current in the read/write head that is transmitted to the computer as 0s and 1s.

CD-ROM

One of the most recent and far-reaching developments in the microcomputer field is the new technology of optical disks. Data are stored on and retrieved from these disks with a laser. One of the most popular kinds of optical disks is called a CD-ROM disc. These discs are similar in concept to the compact discs (CDs) now popular in the music industry. A small 4 3/4-inch CD-ROM disc can store up to 600MB of data. This is equivalent to about 250,000 pages of text or 40,000 images.

These discs are changing the way information is stored, distributed, and accessed. One of the first to be published was *Microsoft's Bookshelf CD-ROM Reference Library*. This CD-ROM disc contains ten of the most widely used reference works, including *The World Almanac and Book of Facts*, *Bartlett's Familiar Quotations*, *The Chicago Manual of Style*, and the *U.S. ZIP Code Directory*. It also includes search and retrieve software, which makes it possible to look for information while working on another program. With just a few keystrokes, you can find information in any of these references and insert it into a document on the screen.

Protecting and Caring for Your Files and Disks

When you enter information into the computer, it is not stored permanently until you save it onto disks. But even then the data are not protected from loss or damage. No one ever heeds advice on this matter until she or he loses important information and has to spend hours or days recreating it. Don't be like everyone else; follow these recommendations before you lose data.

Labeling Your Disks

An unwritten rule among computer users is that an unlabeled disk contains no valuable files. People often do not take the time to check what files, if any, an unlabeled disk contains. Thus the first step when you use a disk is to label it. Always write the disk title, your name, the date, and the operating system version that you are using on the labels.

If you are using 5¼-inch floppy disks, be sure also to fill out labels before you affix them to the disks. If you write on a label that is already on a disk, you can damage the disk if you press down too hard. If you must write on a label that is already on a disk, use a felt-tip pen, and write very gently. Do not apply pressure.

Write-Protecting Your Disks

When you work with files and disks, you can lose work if you make a mistake. To protect important files, write-protect the disk. If a disk is write-protected, you can read files on the disk, but you cannot save files on it, format it, or erase files from it.

- To write-protect a 5¼-inch floppy disk, cover the write-protect notch with a piece of tape. You must use a write-protect tape that light cannot shine through since some drives use a light to determine whether the notch is covered. If you use a transparent tape, the light will shine through the notch just as if it were not covered, and the drive will assume it is not write-protected.
- To write-protect a 3½-inch floppy disk, open the sliding tab in the write-protect window.

Making Backup Copies

Always make backup copies of your important files and disks, and save them a safe distance from your working area. Make sure the same accident cannot happen to both the original disk and its backup copy. The information on the disk is usually worth much more than the disk itself, so don't take chances. You can back up floppy disks using the COPY or XCOPY commands described in this text. Backing up hard disks using the BACKUP command is described in the DOS manual.

Caring for Your Disks

Disks, both hard and floppy, are very reliable storage media. However, the data they contain can be lost or damaged if you do not take a few precautions. Floppy disks are relatively durable under ordinary conditions and have a useful life of about 40 hours' spinning time. But that life can be shortened or abruptly ended by improper handling. Proper

CLASS FILES--ORIGINAL
Your Name / The Date
Formatted with DOS 5

Disk Labels
Disks labels should indicate the type of disk, whether it is an original or backup copy, your name, the date the disk was formatted, and the format used.

Write-Protecting Floppy Disks
You write-protect your disks by taping over the write-protect notch on a 5¼-inch disk or opening the write-protect window on a 3½-inch disk.

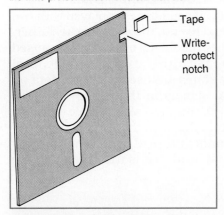

Tape

Write-protect notch

Write-protecting a 5¼-inch disk

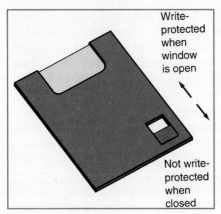

Write-protected when window is open

Not write-protected when closed

Write-protecting a 3½-inch disk

care ensures that disks will accurately store and play back the data you need.

Care of Hard Disk Drives

- *DON'T* drop or jar them. They are very sensitive.
- *DO* use the park program, if necessary, to move the drive's read/write head to a safe place on the disk before moving the computer.

Care of Floppy Disk Drives

- *DON'T* use commercial cleaning kits too often. Overuse can cause problems with the drive.
- *DO* insert the cardboard protectors that came with 5¼-inch disk drives and close the doors when moving the computer.

Care of Floppy Disks

- *DO* keep disks in their protective storage envelopes. These envelopes reduce static buildup, which can attract dust that might scratch the disks.
- *DO* keep disks dry, away from sneezes, coffee, or anything else wet. A wet disk is a ruined disk.
- *DO* prevent disks from getting too hot or too cold. They should be stored at temperatures of 50°-150°F (10°-52°C). Extremes of temperature can destroy a disk's sensitivity, so treat them the same way you treat photographic film; that is, keep them out of direct sunlight, do not leave them in a car exposed to temperature extremes, and so forth.
- *DO* keep disks at least 2 feet away from magnets. The magnets found in copy stands, telephones, radio or stereo speakers, vacuum cleaners, televisions, air conditioners, novelty items, electric motors, or even some cabinet latches can ruin a disk's data.
- *DON'T* touch a disk's recording surface. Handle disks only by their protective covers.
- *DON'T* use a hard-tipped pen to write on a 5¼-inch disk's label that is affixed to the disk. This can crease the disk inside the protective cover and cause you to lose data. Write on the label before affixing it to the disk, or use a felt-tip pen with very light pressure.
- *DON'T* leave a disk in a nonoperating disk drive with the door closed for long periods. Open the drive door to lift the read/write head from the surface of the disk.
- *DON'T* insert or remove a disk from the drive when the disk drive is running (that is, when the drive's light is on).
- *DON'T* bend, fold, or crimp disks.
- *DON'T* use paper clips to attach a floppy disk to a file folder or copy of a printout. Special folders are available that let you keep disks and printed documents together.
- *DON'T* expose disks to static electricity. In dry climates or in heated buildings, static builds up when you walk on carpeted and some other kinds of floors. If you experience shocks when you touch metal objects, you are discharging the static that has built up. If you touch a disk when still charged with this static, you can

damage the data. To prevent this, increase the humidity in the air, use static-proof carpets, or touch something like a lamp to discharge the static before you pick up a disk.

Even with the best of care, floppy disks can last only so long. Close to the end of their useful life, they show their own form of senility by losing information or giving invalid commands. These are signs that it is time to replace them.

▶ E X E R C I S E S

EXERCISE 1

IDENTIFYING PARTS OF A FLOPPY DISK

Sketch a floppy disk used on your system, and then label each of its parts.

EXERCISE 2

PRACTICING INSERTING AND REMOVING FLOPPY DISKS

Practice inserting and removing floppy disks from your system's floppy disk drive. When you have it mastered, summarize the steps for inserting and removing them.

_____

_____

_____

_____

_____

Application Software & the Operating System

After completing this topic, you will be able to:

■ Briefly list and describe the main types of application software programs that you run on a computer
■ Describe the functions of an operating system and graphical user interfaces such as Windows
■ Explain program updates
■ Describe installing programs, and explain why it is necessary

Microcomputers are general-purpose machines with many abilities. You determine their specific applications by the software you use. The computer is like an actor, and the software is like a script. When the actor changes scripts, he or she can perform a different role. By changing software, you can make your computer perform different applications. For example, to use your computer for word processing, you load a word processing program like WordPerfect® into your computer's memory from the disks it is stored on. To use your computer for financial analysis, you load a spreadsheet program like Lotus® 1-2-3®. You do not have to learn programming to make the computer a valuable tool. Instead, you learn how to effectively use these application software programs. Let's look briefly at some of the most popular types of application software and the operating system software that makes them possible.

Word Processing and Desktop Publishing Programs

Word processing programs are used to enter and edit text. They are typically used to prepare memos, letters, reports, manuscripts, contracts, and other types of documents. In addition to entering and editing, these programs allow you to format documents so as to control how they look when printed. For example, you can set margins and tab stops, boldface headings, and automatically print personalized copies of form letters.

Since the introduction of the laser printer, new formatting procedures have become available. For example, you can print in different typestyles and type sizes, and you can combine graphics with text. To take advantage of these new possibilities, a new class of desktop publishing programs was introduced. These programs offer a wide selection of typestyles and make it easy to organize type into columns, add ruled lines, and combine text with graphics on the same page. To use one of these programs, you first enter and edit a document on a word processing program, and then you transfer it to a desktop publishing program where you lay out and design the final document. Increasingly, however, the features offered by desktop publishing

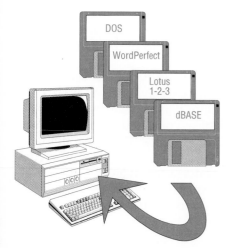

The Computer System's Software
Microcomputers allow you to load a variety of application software into memory so that you can use the same piece of equipment to process words, numbers, data, and graphics.

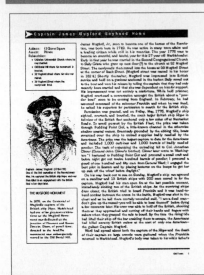

Word Processing and Desktop Publishing Programs

Word processing and desktop publishing programs allow you to create formatted documents that include both text and graphics.

Spreadsheet Programs

A spreadsheet program has a screen divided into rows and columns. Where a row intersects a column, there are rectangular cells, which are used to enter labels, numbers, or formulas that make calculations.

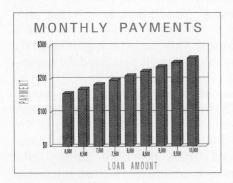

Business Graphs

Business graphs are used to convey a great deal of information in a single picture.

programs are being incorporated into word processing programs, so you can now desktop publish documents without learning a second program.

Spreadsheet Programs

Spreadsheet programs have taken the drudgery out of working with numbers. On a spreadsheet, you quickly create a model of a numeric situation by entering labels, numbers, and formulas. You use the program's built-in features, called functions, to perform complicated calculations, such as the monthly payments due on a loan. You then use the completed model to explore what-if questions. For example, when you change the interest rate for the loan, the spreadsheet instantly recalculates your new monthly payment.

All modern spreadsheet programs include built-in graphics capabilities that allow you to quickly create graphs of any data that you enter into the spreadsheet. If you change the data in the spreadsheet, the graphs based on it change automatically. This makes graphs a usable tool for analysis.

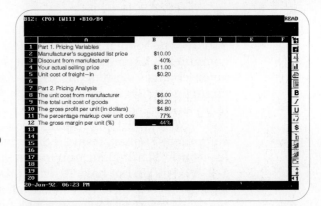

Database Programs

You use database management programs (sometimes called record or file management programs) for tasks as simple as keeping a phone list or as complicated as controlling inventory. These programs allow you to store information in an organized way so that you can retrieve, update, or analyze it when you need to.

These programs do the same things you can do with a set of index cards, but they let you do it faster and more easily. You can store large amounts of information, such as mailing lists, inventory records, or billing and collection information, in tables. You can then sort, edit, add to, or delete from the information in these tables. Database management programs are often used to maintain mailing lists, which are then used automatically to print names and addresses on letters, envelopes, and mailing labels. They are also frequently integrated into other application software, such as word processing and spreadsheet programs.

The Operating System

Although you do your computer work with application programs like word processors and spreadsheets, the heart of the computer's software is another type of software called the operating system. The operating system coordinates activity between you and the computer and between parts of the computer like the keyboard and display screen.

When IBM developed the original IBM PC, it contracted the development of its operating system to Microsoft, which developed an operating system called MS-DOS (Microsoft Disk Operating System). The IBM PC version of this program was named PC-DOS. The PC-DOS version usually runs on IBM PC computers, and the MS-DOS version usually runs on compatibles made by manufacturers other than IBM. These two versions of the operating system are essentially identical in the way they work and the commands you use to operate them; usually they are interchangeable.

Because the operating system coordinates activity between any application program you run and the computer hardware, you must load the operating system into the computer's memory before you load an application program. The primary functions of the operating system are to coordinate, or supervise, the activities of the computer and help you manage your files. When the operating system controls your computer, it performs two main functions: controlling input and output and processing commands.

Controlling Input and Output

The operating system decides where programs and data are stored in the computer's memory and handles communication among the computer's components such as the printer and display screen, the application programs, and you—the user. The operating system controls your computer without your involvement or awareness. In this respect, it is like your body's respiratory system, which keeps you breathing even though you are hardly aware of it.

The Operating System Coordinates Traffic
Intersections without traffic control are confusing. Those with traffic control are more efficient; everyone knows when to stop and when to go. The operating system performs traffic control functions within the computer.

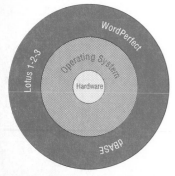

The Operating System and Application Software
The operating system communicates between application software and the hardware. The operating system must always be loaded into the computer's memory before application software such as WordPerfect or 1-2-3 is loaded.

Processing Commands

The command processor portion of the operating system interprets what you enter from the keyboard. In this respect, it is rather like an interpreter. If you spoke only English and tried to carry on a discussion with someone who spoke only French, you both would need an interpreter to translate what was being said so that you could understand each other. The same is true of a computer. When you use an application program, the program's commands are interpreted by the operating system for the hardware. For example, on one program, you might save a file you are working on by pressing [F10] and then pressing [Enter ↵]. On another, you might press [/] [F] [S] and then press [Enter ↵]. The operating system interprets these commands and instructs the disk drive to spin while it copies the file to the disk from the computer's internal memory.

The Operating System Interprets
Command processing is a form of interpreting. The commands you enter on the keyboard are interpreted by the operating system and sent to the computer's central processing unit.

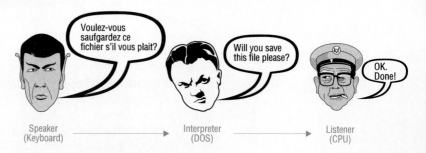

Speaker (Keyboard) → Interpreter (DOS) → Listener (CPU)

File and Disk Management Functions
In addition to the things the operating system does automatically, it contains commands that you use to manage your files and disks. These commands perform tasks such as copying or deleting files and preparing disks for use on your computer. Many of these commands are described in this text.

Graphical User Interfaces

Graphical user interfaces (also called GUIs—pronounced "goo-ees") like Microsoft's Windows make using the computer easier and more efficient. Windows incorporates a graphic display that allows you to choose commands from pull-down menus and to divide the screen into windows in which multiple application programs can be displayed and run at the same time. You can run your favorite spreadsheet in one window and your favorite word processor in another. The program you are currently working on is in the foreground. The other programs, which you are not currently working on, are in the background.

WordPerfect

Icons
Icons are graphic symbols on the screen that you click on with a mouse to run the associated program. For example, if you clicked on the icon shown here, you would load WordPerfect for Windows.

Microsoft Windows
Microsoft Windows, a typical operating system environment, allows you to load more than one program into memory so that you can quickly switch between them. It also allows you to perform many operating system functions, such as copying files, without having to learn the commands usually required.

The Windows Program Manager screen (top) displays icons, graphic symbols that represent programs. To run a program, you just point to it and double click one of the buttons on a mouse.

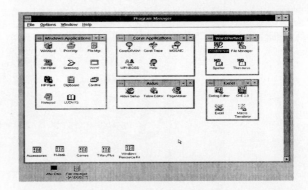

One of the Windows programs is the File Manager (bottom) that displays a graphic tree of the directories on the disk (subdivisions of the disk in which related files are stored) and any files they contain.

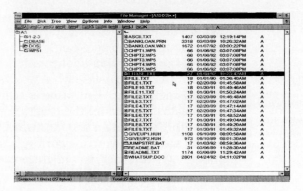

Windows also gives a common look to most programs that are developed to take advantage of its features. For example, it allows you to operate the computer using standardized commands to load programs, call up help, cancel commands, and quit to return to the operating system. This makes it easier to learn new programs because your existing skills are transferable.

Program and Operating System Updates

Companies that publish programs and operating systems generally update them every year or so. Updates (also called upgrades) generally include corrected old features as well as new features that improve the program. To identify new versions, version or release numbers are changed. For example, DOS has been revised several times, so there are versions 3, 3.1, 4, 4.01, and 5 in widespread use. Changes in the decimal number usually indicate relatively minor changes. Changes in the whole number indicate major revisions. For example, version 3.1 is only slightly different from 3.0, but version 5.0 was a big change from version 4.01.

New versions usually add new features. If these just build on the previous version, you need learn only the new features. When faced with a new version, you should be an informed consumer. Find out what features the new program has. If it does not have any that you need, you probably should not buy the new version.

Installing Programs and Operating Systems

Before you actually use a new application program or operating system, you must install it by running an installation program (also called a setup program). The installation process copies the program's or operating system's files to your working disk or disks and customizes it for your system's hardware based on your responses to questions. Installing a program is generally a one-time task unless you change equipment. When you add a new printer or other device, you may have to reinstall the program so that it is aware of the change.

Based on the information you supply about your screen and printer when you install a program, the program then knows what device drivers to use. Drivers are small programs that translate the programmer's generic instructions into instructions for a specific piece of hardware. When a new piece of hardware comes on the market, the programmers of the application software just write a driver for it; they don't have to revise the program itself.

Application software programs generally have a library of device drivers, one for each specific hardware item. If you have a piece of hardware that the program does not include a driver for, you may be unable to use it with the program. Using a printer or display screen without the correct driver can give totally unexpected results. When buying an application software program, always be sure it contains the drivers needed to work with your equipment.

There is often a way around this problem, however. Many pieces of computer hardware are designed to emulate (act like) other brands of the same equipment. Thus, many printers will emulate the Hewlett-Packard LaserJet, and many display screens can emulate IBM's video graphics adapter (VGA). If your program doesn't list the drivers for your printer or screen, but your printer or screen can emulate another, you may be able to install that driver, and the program will run correctly.

°INFOSYSTEMS

"Your hardware doesn't like your software and they both despise your printer!"

Drivers
Reprinted from INFOSYSTEMS, May 1985, © Hitchcock Publishing Company.

THE VIRUSES ARE COMING

- A virus introduced into the computers at several universities counted the number of times it copied itself to other disks. When it had reproduced itself four times, it erased all files on the current disks in the computer.
- ARC, a major shareware program used to compress files so that they take up less space on the disk and can be telecommunicated faster, was altered and then uploaded to bulletin board systems. When it was then downloaded to a user's computer and run, it erased the part of the hard disk that is needed to boot the computer.
- A Christmas message sent over IBM's worldwide network looked up the mailing list of each person it was sent to and then sent itself to all those people. The avalanche of messages that were sent to more and more people slowed down the system and eventually brought it to a halt.
- A virus attached to Aldus's Freehand program displayed a peace message on users' screens on March 2, 1988, the anniversary of Apple's introduction of the Macintosh II. This was the first virus to be distributed in a commercial software program.

Theft of Software

When you walk into a computer store and pay $100 or more for a program, you may think you have bought the program, but usually you would be wrong. You have actually bought the *license*, or right, to use the program and its documentation. The physical materials still belong to the publisher. Read these licenses carefully; they spell out your rights in detail. Most specify that you can use the program only on one computer and cannot make copies for distribution to others. You can, however, make copies for your own use because you should never run the program from the original disk.

Users do not have the right to make copies of software for distribution to others. Doing so infringes on the publisher's copyright and is a federal offense. Called software piracy, this practice costs software companies lost revenues, and they are increasingly taking legal action to prevent the distribution, sale, and use of these disks, especially in colleges and large corporations. Colleges and corporations are even being held accountable for the actions of students and employees who illegally copy programs.

A site license allows a school or company either to run programs on networks without having a copy for each computer or to make a limited number of copies for use within a single department or location. Site licenses reduce the company's total software costs, lessen the likelihood of violating the publisher's legal rights, and make it easier on all network users because they do not need individual copies of the program.

Viruses

One of the fastest growing problems in the microcomputer field is the introduction of viruses by antisocial users. A virus is a small program, either stored on a disk by itself or appended to an existing file called a Trojan horse. When the file is loaded or the Trojan horse program is run, the virus loads itself into the computer's memory. Once there, it can secretly attach itself to other files or programs or store itself on any other disks run on the computer, including the hard disk. What happens next depends on the intent of the vandal who created the virus:

- The virus may cause problems immediately.
- It may count specific occurrences, for example, how many times it is copied, and then cause damage.
- It may look at the computer's clock and cause damage on a specific date.
- It may reproduce itself and then cause damage. Like a biological virus, a computer virus can infect other files and then spread from them.

The number of instances in which viruses cause damage is increasing. Once introduced, viruses are hard to detect and remove. For individual users, the best defense is to use only commercial programs and not to exchange files with other users. Using a virus scan program will help you detect the presence of viruses on your system.

EXERCISE 1

ATTENDING A DEMONSTRATION

Application software is demonstrated in college labs, in computer stores, and in computer groups. Try to attend a demonstration of any program to see how it operates, and then summarize your observations.

EXERCISE 2

READING A REVIEW

Obtain a copy of a recent computer magazine and read a review of any new program. List its main applications, and briefly describe some of the features that the reviewer thought important.

EXERCISE 3

READING A LICENSE AGREEMENT

Ask the person in charge of your computer lab to show you a license agreement covering a software program that you will be using. Read the agreement, list the rights it gives you, and list the things it prohibits.

REVIEW

- Bytes can be indicated using the shorthand terms kilobyte (KB) for thousands, megabyte (MB) for millions, gigabyte for billions, or terabyte for trillions. They are calculated by raising the number 2 (for the two possible states of the transistor) to a power. For example, 2^{18} is 262,144 bytes or 262 kilobytes (rounded off to 256 for most purposes).

- The central processing unit (CPU) coordinates the computer's activities and performs arithmetic and logical calculations. The microcomputer's CPU is a microprocessor.

- Microprocessors come in full featured versions (dx) and more limited but less expensive versions (sx).

- There are two basic types of internal memory: read-only memory (ROM) and random-access memory (RAM). ROM is unchangeable, but your programs and data are stored in RAM. Because you can change the data in RAM, it is called volatile memory.

- Data can enter and leave the computer through ports. Serial ports send data a bit at a time, and parallel ports send data a byte at a time.

- Many computers have expansion slots into which you can plug boards to improve the performance of your system.

- WYSIWYG displays show a document on the screen almost exactly as it will appear when printed.

- Off-Line/On-Line connects and disconnects the printer from the computer, and Form Feed advances the paper out of the printer.

- The most common external storage devices are floppy and hard disks. Hard disks not only store more data but also allow you to store and retrieve it faster than floppy disks do.

- To protect your files, you should label your disks, make backup copies, and write-protect the disks when executing commands that could damage the files.

- The operating system controls the computer's operations and must always be loaded before you load an application program.

- When new features are added to an existing program, it is released by the publisher as an update.

QUESTIONS

FILL IN THE BLANK

1. The smallest unit of information in a computer is the _____.
2. Bytes contain _____ bits.
3. The abbreviation for a kilobyte is _____ and for a megabyte it is _____.

4. The abbreviation CPU stands for _____ _____ _____.

5. Memory in the computer where you store your files and programs when you are using them is called _____.

6. The port where data are sent through a bit at a time is called a _____ port.

7. The port where data are sent through a byte at a time is called a _____ port.

8. When a display screen can display only a fixed set of characters, it is called a _____ display.

9. When a display screen can show a photograph, it is called a _____ display.

10. If the screen shows a document almost exactly as it will be when printed, it is called a _____ display.

11. To change the style of type in a printed document, your printer must have more than one _____.

12. Installing a program tells it which _____ to use to communicate with devices such as printers and display screens.

MATCH THE COLUMNS

1. DOS	__ [Esc]
2. The smallest unit of computer information	__ [CapsLock]
	__ Byte
3. Contains 8 bits	__ An operating system
4. CPU	__ Read-only memory
5. Storage for documents	__ Ports
6. Memory you cannot change	__ Expansion slots and boards
7. Attach peripherals	__ Central processing unit
8. Expand the computer's capabilities	__ [Enter ←]
	__ Determine the style of type you can print with
9. Enters uppercase letters	
10. Cancels commands	__ Bit
11. Enters commands	__ [← Bksp]
12. Deletes characters	__ Random-access memory
13. Fonts	

WRITE OUT THE ANSWERS

1. What is the difference between a bit and a byte?
2. Describe the differences between RAM and ROM.
3. What is the function of a port? List the two kinds of ports on a computer, and describe the basic difference between them.
4. What is the purpose of the expansion slots inside a computer? What can they be used for?
5. What does it mean when you say a key toggles?
6. What is the difference between a graphics display and a character display?
7. What is the primary difference among CGA, EGA, VGA, and XGA?
8. What are fonts?
9. What does it mean to say a printer is on line or off line? What switch on the printer do you use to take the printer off line and then put it back on line?
10. What switch on the printer do you press to advance the paper to the top of the next sheet?
11. List and briefly describe the two main types of external storage media and devices.
12. When you are going to move a microcomputer, what step should you take to protect the hard disk drive?
13. What is the purpose of the write-protect notch or window on a floppy disk? What can you do when the disk is write-protected, and what can you not do? What can you do when it is not write-protected?
14. Why does a computer need an operating system?
15. What are the operating system's utility programs used for?
16. Do you think it is legal or ethical to copy disks when a publisher has asked you not to? Why or why not?
17. When you buy a program, do you usually buy all rights to it?

PROJECTS

PROJECT 1

LOCATING LIBRARY RESOURCES

When learning about computers, you can find much useful and interesting information in magazines and newspapers devoted to the field. Most libraries subscribe to at least some of the major computer magazines. Visit the library, and list the computer magazines or other periodicals to which your library subscribes. Read some of the articles and ads in these magazines to become familiar with computer terms and applications.

❏ *PC World* ❏ *PC Magazine*
❏ *MacWorld* ❏ *BYTE*
❏ *PC Week* ❏ *InfoWorld*
❏ _____ ❏ _____
❏ _____ ❏ _____

Read a review in one of the computer magazines on a desktop or laptop computer, and fill in the information below.

Manufacturer: _____
Model: _____
Size of internal memory (RAM): _____
Type of microprocessor: _____
Type of display (CRT or flat panel): _____

PROJECT 2

VIEWING A VIDEO

Many videocassettes have been developed to introduce users to specific computers. Visit your library, learning center, or computer lab to see if any are available for you to view. You might also find one in a local video store. If you do, you can share the rental cost with other students and view the video together.

PROJECT 3

ATTENDING A USER GROUP MEETING

Many towns have computer groups that hold periodic meetings. Frequently, these groups are divided into smaller groups called Special Interest Groups, or SIGs, where particular computer systems or programs are discussed. Ask around to see if there is a computer group in your area, and if so, attend one of its meetings.

Getting Started with DOS

DOS—An Overview

After completing this topic, you will be able to:
- Load DOS on a floppy or hard disk system
- Determine the version number of DOS that your system is running
- Quit DOS and turn off your equipment

To use a computer, you must first load the operating system. This is called booting the system. The term *booting* comes from the expression "pulling oneself up by one's bootstraps." Once the operating system is loaded, you can load your application programs or use the operating system's commands to manage your files and disks.

If your computer is off, you load the operating system by turning it on. When you do so, the computer automatically looks to the startup drive for the operating system files that it needs to start up.

- On a floppy disk system, the startup drive is drive A, so you have to insert a disk that contains the operating system files into that drive.
- On a hard disk system, the startup drive is drive C, but the computer still looks to drive A first. Therefore, before you turn on a hard disk system, be sure to open the door to drive A or eject the disk so that the program does not try to load the operating system from that drive (see the section "Things That Can Go Wrong").

If the files it needs to start are on the disk in the startup drive, that disk is called a *system disk*. If the files are not on the disk in the startup drive, an error message is displayed, and the system will not boot.

Turning a computer on to boot it is called a cold boot. However, you can also reboot a computer if it is already on—called warm booting. To warm-boot the system, you hold down [Ctrl] and [Alt] and then press [Del]. (This command is usually written out as **Ctrl-Alt-Del**.). Warm booting clears all data from the computer's memory and has almost the same effect as turning the computer off and then back on again. You normally use this procedure only when you encounter a problem with your system. Whenever possible, you should exit any application program you are using before warm booting your system, or you may lose data.

In this tutorial, you take a quick guided tour of some of the most commonly used DOS procedures. You load DOS, check which version you are using, format a disk so that you can store your own work on it, explore directories, and copy files. Everything you do here will be explained in much greater detail later in this text, so relax. The purpose of this Jump-Start Tutorial is to get you over the initial hurdle of using DOS and to make it possible for you to perform basic procedures should the need arise at home, at work, or in other courses.

To load DOS on some systems, such as those connected to networks or with special startup menus, you follow procedures specific to your system. In these cases, ask your instructor how to display the DOS command prompt, and then start this tutorial at the section headed "Changing the Command Prompt."

GETTING STARTED

1. If your computer is on, turn it off. The location of the On/Off switch varies, but it may be located on the right side of the computer toward the rear.
2. Before proceeding:
    - If you are working on a hard disk system, open the door to drive A or eject the disk in that drive. Drive A is the name of the floppy drive if there is only one. If there are two (or more) drives, drive A is usually the one on the top or on the left.
    - If you are working on a floppy disk system, insert the DOS disk into drive A. If there are two (or more) drives, drive A is usually the one on the top or on the left. (On some systems, there may be more than one DOS disk. If you are working on such a system, the disk you use to boot the computer might be named the DOS startup, boot, or system disk. If you are unsure of which disk to use, ask.)

LOADING THE OPERATING SYSTEM

3. Turn on the computer. In a few moments, the computer may beep, and then drive A spins, and its light comes on while the operating system is loaded. If there is no disk in drive A, the computer looks to drive C for the program if the system contains a hard disk drive.
    - If a list of files is displayed, and the screen has the title *MS-DOS Shell*, *IBM DOS Shell*, or *Start Programs*, press F3 to display the command prompt.
    - If nothing appears on your screen, your display screen may not be on. On some systems, the display screen has a separate On/Off switch.
    - If your computer does not have a clock that is set automatically, in a moment the prompt reads *Enter new date:*. If this prompt appears, refer to the section "Entering or Changing the Date and Time" in the Quick Reference section of this topic.

    The command prompt appears and should read *C:\>*, *C>*, *C:\DOS>*, *A:\>*, *A>*, or something similar. This prompt indicates that DOS has been loaded.

CHANGING THE COMMAND PROMPT

4. If your command prompt does not read *C:\>*, *C:\DOS>*, or *A:\>*, type **PROMPT PG** and press ⎡Enter ⏎⎤ so that it does (although the *DOS* part may be different).

CHECKING THE VERSION NUMBER

5. Type **VER** and press ⎡Enter ⏎⎤ to display the version number of the operating system you are using. Write it down so that you don't forget it. The commands you use vary somewhat depending on which version of DOS your system is running.

FORMATTING A DATA DISK

6. Locate a blank disk that **DOES NOT** contain any valuable files. The command you are about to use effectively erases all data from the disk.

7. Insert your disks as follows:
   ■ On a hard disk system, insert the blank disk into drive A.
   ■ On a floppy disk system with two disk drives, insert the DOS disk into drive A and the blank disk into drive B.

8. Set your drives as follows:
   ■ On a hard disk system, type **C:** and press ⎡Enter ⏎⎤ to change the default drive to drive C. The command prompt should read *C:\>* or *C:\DOS>*.
   ■ On a floppy disk system, type **A:** and press ⎡Enter ⏎⎤ to change the default drive to drive A. The command prompt should read *A:\>*.

9. Enter the FORMAT command as follows:
   ■ On a hard disk system, type **FORMAT A:** and press ⎡Enter ⏎⎤.
   ■ On a floppy disk system, type **FORMAT B:** and press ⎡Enter ⏎⎤.
   In a moment, a prompt asks you to insert a disk into the drive you entered in the FORMAT command and press or strike ⎡Enter ⏎⎤ when ready. You already inserted the disks in a previous step. (If you get the message *Bad command or filename*, or something similar, ask your instructor on what disk or in which directory the FORMAT.COM file can be found, and insert that disk or ask how you change to that directory.)

10. Press ⎡Enter ⏎⎤, and the drive spins as it formats the disk. (On DOS 4 and later versions, a message on the screen keeps you posted on the progress.) When the message reads *Format complete*, the drive stops.

11. If you are using DOS 4 or a later version, you are prompted to enter a volume label. Type your last name (abbreviate to 11 characters if necessary), and press ⎡Enter ⏎⎤ to continue.)

12. When the prompt reads *Format another (Y/N)?*, press ⎡N⎤ and then press ⎡Enter ⏎⎤.

EXPLORING YOUR STUDENT RESOURCE DISK

13. Insert the *Student Resource Disk* into drive A. (The *Student Resource Disk* is a special disk that contains all the files you need to complete the tutorials and exercises in this text.)

LOOKING AHEAD: DIRECTORIES

Disks can store a lot of files. To keep them organized, experienced users divide the disk into directories that are like file folders in which related files can be stored. Knowing which directory a file is in is important since you may not be able to run a program or copy a file unless you do. Directories are discussed in detail in Topic 14. For now, think of them as an address. Just as you may live in San Francisco in the state of California, a file may be stored in a directory named DOS on a drive named C.

LOOKING BACK: WRITE-PROTECTION

As you saw in Topic 4, a disk must not be write-protected when you copy files to it.
- To remove write-protection from a 5¼-inch floppy disk, remove the tape covering the write-protect notch.
- To remove write-protection from a 3½-inch floppy disk, close the sliding tab in the write-protect window.

14. Type **A:** and press ⏎ Enter to change the default drive to A, and the command prompt reads *A:\\>*.
15. Type **DIR** and press ⏎ Enter to list the directories on the disk. Directories are like file folders in which you can store related files. They are used to organize your work and programs on the disk. You can tell 1-2-3, DBASE, DOS, EXCHANGE, and WP51 are directories because they are followed by the notation *<DIR>*.
16. Type **CD \\DOS** and press ⏎ Enter. The prompt changes to *A:\\DOS>* to indicate that DOS on drive A is the current directory.
17. Type **DIR** and press ⏎ Enter to display a list of the files in the DOS directory along with information about each file. The list is too long to be displayed on the screen, so the topmost files scroll off the top. However, notice how each file has a name such as WHATSUP, an extension such as DOC, a size (in bytes), a date, and a time.
18. Type **DIR/W** and press ⏎ Enter to display the filenames in five columns without additional information so that more names can be displayed at one time.
19. Type **CD \\DBASE** and press ⏎ Enter to move to the DBASE directory.
20. Type **DIR** and press ⏎ Enter to display a list of the files in that directory.
21. Type **CD \\DOS** and press ⏎ Enter to return to the DOS directory.
22. Type **DIR *.DOC** and press ⏎ Enter. The command told DOS to list any file with a period followed by the three letters DOC.

COPYING FILES

23. Type **COPY *.* A:** and press ⏎ Enter to copy all the files from the DOS directory to A:\\, the topmost directory on the disk—called the *root directory*. Files are listed on the screen as they are copied, and when all have been copied, the command prompt reappears. The *.* (called star-dot-star) part of the command uses wildcards to tell DOS "all files."
24. Type **DIR** and press ⏎ Enter to see that all the files are still in the DOS directory.
25. Type **CD ** and press ⏎ Enter to move back up to the root directory. The command prompt should change to A:\\> to indicate that you are there.
26. Type **DIR** and press ⏎ Enter to see that copies of all the files that were in the DOS directory are now in the root directory.

FINISHING UP

27. Either continue to the next activity or quit for the day. To quit, remove your disks from the drives and turn off the computer.

QUICK REFERENCE

You have to load the operating system only once during a session. If you are already running an application program, you use the application program's Quit or Exit command to return to the operating system or the menu from which you loaded the program.

→ KEY/Strokes

Loading DOS

1. Set your disk drives as follows:
   - To boot from a hard disk, open the door to drive A or eject any disk from the drive.
   - To boot from a floppy disk, insert a system disk (a disk with the DOS files needed to start up the computer) into drive A.
2. Turn on the computer. What happens next depends on how your system has been set up. Any of the following events may happen:
   - If your system's clock is not set automatically, you are prompted to enter the date and time each time you turn it on. If you are prompted to do so, see the section "Entering or Changing the Date and Time."
   - If your system is connected to a network, or has been customized, a menu may appear on the screen listing actions you can take.
   - The command prompt may appear and will normally be *A>* or *A:\>* if you booted from a floppy disk or *C:\>* if you booted from a hard disk drive. However, the command prompt can be customized, so it may be different on your system. The command prompt tells you that DOS has been loaded, that the default, or active, disk drive is drive A or C; and that the drive is ready to receive commands. From this command prompt, you can execute all DOS commands or start application programs such as WordPerfect, Lotus 1-2-3, or dBASE.
   - The DOS Shell, a menu-operated screen, may appear on systems using DOS 4 or later versions. To display the command prompt from this Shell, press F3 .

The DOS 5 Shell

DOS 4 and later versions contain a Shell with pull-down menus you can use to execute commands. This illustration shows the screen that appears when the DOS 5 Shell is loaded.

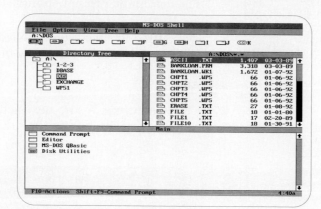

Network Menus

Many computers are connected to networks so that they can communicate with one another. On these systems, special screens may appear that list programs you can run or commands you can execute.

MILITARY TIME

Versions of DOS prior to 4.0 do not recognize **a** and **p** after the time to indicate a.m. or p.m. With those versions, to set the computer's clock accurately in the afternoon or evening, so that its date will change at midnight, you must use military time. Military time is based on the 24-hour clock. In military time, the hours from 1 a.m. until noon have the same names as they do with the 12-hour clock. But at 1 p.m., the hour is 13:00 (called "thirteen hundred hours"); 2 p.m. is fourteen hundred hours; and so on until midnight, which is zero hours, when the sequence begins again.

Entering or Changing the Date and Time

When you first turn on some computers, you are prompted to enter the date and time. Entering the correct date and time is important because the computer's clock date-and-time-marks files that you save. The clock is also used by some programs to enter dates and times into files and to display them on the screen.

If you are prompted to enter the date, type it in the format MM-DD-YY, where MM (month) is a number from 1 to 12, DD (day) is a number from 1 to 31, and YY (year) is a number from 80 to 99 or from 1980 to 1999. For example, to enter the date January 10, 1993, type 1-10-93 and press Enter⏎.

To enter the time when prompted to do so, use the format HH:MM, where HH (hours) is a number between 0 and 23, and MM (minutes) is a number between 0 and 59. For example, to set the clock to 1:30 p.m., type **13:30** (for military time—see box) and press Enter⏎. If you are using DOS 4 or later, you could also enter the time as 1:30p (for p.m.).

Things That Can Go Wrong

It is not at all likely that anything you type on a computer will really harm the system, but it is easy to make mistakes that affect your own work. That's why you should always keep backup copies of important files and take care to follow the directions in this text as you enter commands that are new to you. Here are some problems to look out for when working with DOS:

- When you boot an IBM computer system, you may see the error message *Non-System disk or disk error* (or a similar message on compatible computers). This appears when you turn on the computer with a disk in drive A that does not contain the operating system files that the computer needs. If you get this message, insert the DOS disk into drive A or open the drive's door if it is a hard disk system, and press Enter⏎.
- The message *Bad command or filename* appears when you type a command incorrectly or when DOS cannot find the file you have tried to run. If you get this prompt, retype the command, or find a disk with the DOS utility program that you want to use.
- If you make a typo and notice it before you press Enter⏎, press ← Bksp to delete it, and then retype it.
- If you or the computer addresses a drive (for example, type **A:** and press Enter⏎) and the drive doesn't contain a disk, a message tells you the computer is not ready reading the drive and then offers you options to *abort, retry, fail,* or *ignore* (although the choices vary depending on the version of DOS you are using).
  - *Abort* cancels the command and returns you to the command prompt (or Shell).
  - *Retry* retries the command, perhaps after you have closed a drive door or inserted a disk.
  - *Fail* cancels the current portion of the command and then continues.
  - *Ignore* ignores the problem and continues processing the command.
- To cancel a command in progress, press Ctrl-C or Ctrl-Break.

Quitting DOS

When you are done for the day, you should always exit the program you are using to return to the operating system, and then:

- Open the floppy disk drive doors or eject the disks in the drives so that the disk drives' read/write heads don't leave indentations in the disks' surfaces.
- Remove your disks from the disk drives to prevent their loss, increase security, and ensure that no one mistakenly erases them.
- Turn off the computer or use the display monitor's controls to dim the screen so that an image will not be "burned" into its phosphor surface.

On some systems, after turning your computer off, you should wait 20 to 30 seconds before turning it back on. Some systems will not reboot without this pause. If you turn one of these systems back on too quickly, nothing happens.

▶ E X E R C I S E S

EXERCISE 1

LOADING DOS ON YOUR OWN SYSTEM

Many computers are now networked or have other special startup procedures. If your system is one of these, list the steps here that you use to access the DOS command prompt so that you have it for future reference.

1. _____
   _____
2. _____
   _____
3. _____
   _____
4. _____
   _____
5. _____
   _____

EXERCISE 2

IDENTIFYING YOUR SYSTEM'S FLOPPY DISK DRIVES

If your system has more than one floppy disk drive, make a sketch of them and label them A, B, and so on. Use this sketch for later reference when you are asked to insert a disk into a specific floppy disk drive.

Executing Commands

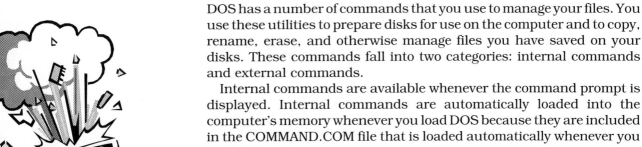

After completing this topic, you will be able to:
- Describe the difference between internal and external commands
- Execute commands from the command prompt
- Print the screen display

Relax!
There is almost nothing that you can do from the keyboard that will damage the system or cause serious problems. If there were, it would be the system designer's fault and not yours.

DOS has a number of commands that you use to manage your files. You use these utilities to prepare disks for use on the computer and to copy, rename, erase, and otherwise manage files you have saved on your disks. These commands fall into two categories: internal commands and external commands.

Internal commands are available whenever the command prompt is displayed. Internal commands are automatically loaded into the computer's memory whenever you load DOS because they are included in the COMMAND.COM file that is loaded automatically whenever you boot the system.

External commands are stored on the DOS disk or hard disk until you need them. These commands are used less often than internal commands. Not loading them into memory until they are needed leaves room for other programs and data.

External commands are little more than small programs that are loaded into the computer's memory and then executed when you type their name and press Enter←. If you enter an external command and its program is not on the disk in the drive, the computer displays an error message indicating you have used a bad command. When this occurs, you first make sure you entered the correct command. If you did, you then use the DIR command (which you'll learn more about later) to check if the command's file is on the disk and, if not, locate the disk it is on. If you use an external command frequently, copying the appropriate program file from the DOS disk onto an application program disk may be helpful.

EXTERNAL COMMANDS ON HARD DISK SYSTEMS

This tutorial and all other DOS activities in this text assume that your hard disk system's AUTOEXEC.BAT file contains a PATH command listing the directory in which the DOS program files are stored. All hard disk external commands are given in this text without specifying the location of the DOS files needed to execute them.

Usually DOS files are stored in a directory of their own on the hard disk. As you may recall, directories are like file folders in which you can store related files. If you are working on a hard disk system, ask your instructor where the DOS files are stored and write down the name of the directory because you may need to know it to complete the activities in this text. Now, let's look at two ways you can execute DOS's external commands.

1. The best way to execute commands is to have the DOS directory listed in the PATH command in the AUTOEXEC.BAT file that the system reads when you boot it. Type **C:** and press [Enter ←] to make drive C the default drive. Then, type **C:** and press [Enter ←] to be sure you are in the topmost directory of drive C. Finally, type **TYPE AUTOEXEC.BAT** and press [Enter ←]. If you get the message *File not found*, or if no line in the file begins with the word *PATH*, your system does not have a PATH command, so proceed to Step 2. If a line in the file does begin with *PATH*, look to see if the name of your DOS directory is listed on the line. For example, if your DOS files are in a directory named DOS, one part of the line should read *C:\DOS*. If your directory is listed, you can execute DOS external commands without any concern for the directory they are stored in. The PATH command tells DOS to look for them in the listed directory.

2. If your system does not have a PATH command, you have to either be in the DOS directory to execute an external command or refer to the directory in the command. For example, to move into the DOS directory, assuming it is named DOS, type **CD \DOS** and press [Enter ←].

LOOKING AHEAD: THE AUTOEXEC.BAT FILE

When you boot your system, one of the first things it does is look for a file on the startup drive named AUTOEXEC.BAT. This file contains commands that are then executed before the command prompt is displayed.

▶ TUTORIAL

In this tutorial, you experiment with some basic commands. (To execute the CHKDSK command described in this tutorial, you will need a copy of the DOS utility file CHKDSK.COM or CHKDSK.EXE.) If your system uses more than one DOS disk, ask which disk it is on.

GETTING STARTED

1. Load DOS so that the command prompt is displayed.
2. Insert the original write-protected copy of the *Student Resource Disk* into drive A.
3. Type **A:** and press [Enter ←], and the command prompt indicates that drive A is the default drive.
4. Check that the printer is on and has paper in it.

EXECUTING SOME INTERNAL COMMANDS

5. Type **DATE** and press [Enter ←] to display the current date and a prompt asking you to enter a new date.
6. Press [Enter ←], and the date is left unchanged. The command prompt reappears.
7. Type **TIME** and press [Enter ←] to display the current time and a prompt asking you to enter a new time.
8. Press [Enter ←], and the time is left unchanged. The command prompt reappears.
9. Type **CLS** and press [Enter ←] to clear the screen and move the command prompt to the upper left corner of the screen.

LOOKING AHEAD: THE CHKDSK COMMAND

You use the CHKDSK command to find out how much space is still available on a disk and in the computer's memory. This command also tells you if all the files on your disk are stored correctly. If it finds that they are scattered, you will see a message that files are in noncontiguous blocks. This is discussed in Topic 19.

10. Type **DIR** and press $\boxed{\text{Enter} \leftarrow}$ to list the names of the files on the disk.

11. If you are working on a floppy disk system (leave things as is on a hard disk system):
    - Move the *Student Resource Disk* to drive B.
    - Type **B:** and press $\boxed{\text{Enter} \leftarrow}$ to change the default drive to B.
    - Insert the DOS disk containing the DOS utility file CHKDSK.COM or CHKDSK.EXE into drive A. (Ask your instructor if you are not sure of which disk to use.)

12. Enter a command as follows:
    - On a hard disk system, type **CHKDSK** and press $\boxed{\text{Enter} \leftarrow}$.
    - On a floppy disk system, type **A:CHKDSK** and press $\boxed{\text{Enter} \leftarrow}$.

    The screen indicates how much room is on your disk and in your internal memory and how much of it has been used. If you get a message that tells you it is a bad command or filename, see the box "External Commands on Hard Disk Systems" in the introduction to this topic

13. Type **TYPE WHATSUP.DOC** and press $\boxed{\text{Enter} \leftarrow}$. The contents of the file are scrolled up the screen too fast to read them.

14. If you are working on a floppy disk system, insert the DOS disk containing the DOS utility file MORE.COM into drive A. (It's probably on the same disk you inserted into drive A earlier.)

15. Enter a command as follows: (The | character is the split vertical bar($\vdots$) on the backslash (\ ) key. You must press $\boxed{\text{Shift}}$ to enter it.)
    - On a hard disk system, type **TYPE WHATSUP.DOC |MORE** and press $\boxed{\text{Enter} \leftarrow}$.
    - On a floppy disk system, type **TYPE WHATSUP.DOC |A:MORE** and press $\boxed{\text{Enter} \leftarrow}$.

    The list of Bugs Bunny films directed by Chuck Jones scrolls onto the screen until the screen is full. Then, the screen pauses, and the prompt - - *More* - - is displayed at the bottom of the screen.

16. Press any key to scroll through the document a screenful at a time until the command prompt reappears.

17. Either continue to the next activity or quit for the day. To quit, remove your disks from the drive and turn off the computer.

LOOKING AHEAD: SPECIFYING PATHS TO A PROGRAM

The CHKDSK command is an external command, so DOS needs to know where this file is located when you execute the command. If it is not on the default drive, you have to specify which drive it is on. If the file is on drive A, you indicate its location by specifying A:CHKDSK. The A: part of the command is called a path since it tells DOS what path to follow to find the file.

LOOKING AHEAD: THE MORE COMMAND

When you display directories or files from DOS, they may scroll off the top of the screen too fast to be read. In these cases, you can use the |MORE command to pause the screen whenever the screen is full. The command then displays a message - - *More* - - and you press any key to scroll to the next screenful of data.

> **QUICK REFERENCE**

To execute commands, you type them in and press $\boxed{\text{Enter} \leftarrow}$. However, you can also save time by executing a command you have used previously without having to retype it or by editing it into a new form.

Executing Commands

To execute commands from the command prompt, you type the name of the command and press [Enter←]. When the command is finished executing, the command prompt reappears.

When you type commands, there are certain conventions that you must follow. Getting used to these conventions takes practice. If you do not follow them exactly, an error message is displayed, but no harm is done. When entering commands, keep the following conventions in mind:

- You can use uppercase, lowercase, or any combination of case. For example, when checking a disk, you can type **CHKDSK**, **chkdsk**, or **Chkdsk**, and the computer accepts them all.
- Parts of many commands must be separated from each other by *delimiters*. Delimiters, which are like punctuation marks in English, indicate where parts of a command begin or end. DOS delimiters include spaces, colons, and slashes.
  - Spaces should not be used at times. For example, you do not enter spaces between the drive, path, and filename. You type **B:\<***filename***>** not **B: \<***filename***>**. The colon and backslash act as the delimiters.
  - Spaces should be used at other times. For example, when displaying a directory of a disk other than the default, you type **DIR B:** not **DIRB:**.
- Many commands can include optional *switches* that modify them. These switches must be separated from the command by a delimiter. For example, to display the directory of a disk in drive B across the screen, you type **DIR B:/W**.

Responding to Prompts

When working with DOS and application programs, you often encounter prompts, which are simply requests for you to supply the computer with information it needs. Some prompts, like the command prompt, are cryptic. Others are more helpful; for example, a prompt may ask *Insert new diskette for drive A Press Enter to continue*. To enter responses to these prompts, you take the requested actions. Some commands then continue automatically. With others, you have to enter a response like **Y** or **N** (for Yes or No), and then you sometimes have to confirm that response by pressing [Enter←] to continue.

Editing Commands

When you type commands, you might make a mistake, or you might want to repeat the same command, perhaps with a few changes. DOS has editing keys and commands that allow you to do each of these things.

To cancel a command that you have not yet executed by pressing [Enter←], press [Ctrl]-[Break] or [Ctrl]-[C] (hold down [Ctrl] while you press the second key) to return to the command prompt.

When entering a command, you can press [←Bksp] to delete typos. To cancel a partially entered command, press [Esc]. This places a backslash (\) character at the end of the current line and moves the cursor down one line ready for a new command. At this point, you can either press [Enter←] to return to the command prompt, or enter a new command and press [Enter←].

GETTING HELP

On-line help was added to DOS beginning with DOS 4, but in that version it is available only from the Shell. Beginning with DOS 5, you can obtain help when working from the command prompt. Microsoft customizes DOS 5 for its customers so versions from Microsoft, IBM, Compaq, and others may vary slightly from one another. On the original Microsoft version, the following commands work as described. On other versions, you may find slight differences but the following commands should get you pointed in the right direction.

- For brief help, type **HELP** and press [Enter←] to display a list of commands with a brief description of each. Since all the commands cannot be listed at once, the screen periodically pauses. To see the next screen, press any key. To return directly to the command prompt at any point, press [Ctrl]-[C].
- For detailed help on a specific command, type **HELP** <*command*> and press [Enter←]. For example, for help on the DIR command, type **HELP DIR** and press [Enter←].

The last command you typed is stored in a buffer, a small area of memory used to store keystrokes. You can recall the command from that buffer to edit it. There are many commands you can use to do so, but the two most popular are [F1], which displays the previous command one character at a time, and [F3], which displays the complete command. Once the command is displayed on the command line, you can press [Enter←] to execute it or press [←Bksp] to delete characters and type new ones at the end of the line.

DOS 5 added a new feature called DOSKEY that makes it easy to repeat or edit previous commands. To use this feature, type **DOSKEY** and press [Enter←] to load this external command. Once it has been loaded, it stores each command you use so that you can redisplay any of them on the command line. To display a list of all commands that have been saved, type **DOSKEY /HISTORY** and press [Enter←] or press [F7].

To display a specific command so that you can repeat it or edit it, press [↑] or [PgDn] to display the command you used most recently, or press [PgUp] to display the oldest command you used. Once you have displayed a command, you can use [↑] and [↓] to scroll back and forward through them.

Once the command you want is displayed on the command line, you can press [Enter←] to execute it, or you can edit it by moving the cursor through the command and inserting or deleting characters. To delete a character, you move the cursor under it, and type a new character or press [Del]. You can also move the cursor to the right of a character, and press [←Bksp] to delete it. To insert characters, press [Ins] to turn on insert mode, and the cursor should change shape to indicate that you are in insert mode. Move the cursor to where you want to insert one or more characters, and type them in. The characters above the cursor and those to its right move aside to make room for the new characters. The commands used most frequently with DOSKEY are described in the table "DOSKEY Edit Commands."

DOSKEY EDIT COMMANDS

Key	Description
[↑] or [PgDn]	Displays the command you used most recently.
[PgUp]	Displays the oldest command you used.
[↑] and [↓]	Scrolls back and forward through the displayed commands.
[←] or [→]	Moves the cursor left or right one character.
[Ctrl]-[←] or [Ctrl]-[→]	Moves the cursor left or right one word.
[Home] or [End]	Moves the cursor to the beginning or end of line.
[Esc]	Removes the command from the display.
[F7]	Displays all stored commands as a numbered list.
[Alt]-[F7]	Erases all stored commands.
[F8]	Searches for the stored command you want. Type the first few characters in the command, and press [F8] to display the most recent version you used. Press [F8] to cycle through any other versions being stored.
[F9]	Prompts you to type the number of a command you want to repeat. (Use [F7] to find numbers.)

TIP

If numbers appear when you press the arrow keys on the numeric keypad, the [NumLock] key is engaged. To disengage it, press it once.

EXERCISE 1

PRINTING THE SCREEN

In some cases, your instructor may want a printed record of the commands you execute in the activities in this text. If you are requested to submit printed results, there are two ways to do so. You can print the current screen, or you can turn on printing so that everything that appears on your screen is printed. Complete this exercise only if your instructor approves since the commands discussed here can cause problems on some systems.

1. Be sure your printer is on. If you use one of the commands in this exercise when your printer isn't on, your system may "hang" and not accept keyboard input until you turn the printer on.
2. Type **DIR/W** and press Enter↵ to display a list of the files on the disk.
3. Press ⇧Shift-PrtScr (or just PrtScr on an enhanced keyboard) to print what is currently displayed on the screen. (To see the printout on some printers, you may have to press On Line to take the printer off line, FF for Form Feed, and then On Line again to put the printer back on line.)
4. Press Ctrl-PrtScr to turn on screen printing so that you will have a running, printed record of what you do while working from the command prompt.
5. Repeat the tutorial at the beginning of this topic. When finished, press Ctrl-PrtScr again to turn printing off.

EXERCISE 2

EXECUTING INTERNAL AND EXTERNAL COMMANDS

In this exercise, you practice executing internal and external commands. All the commands that you enter here are similar to those you entered in this topic's tutorial. If you need help on a command, refer to the tutorial to see how you executed it there.

1. Insert your disks as follows:
   - On a hard disk system, insert the *Student Resource Disk* into drive A.
   - On a floppy disk system, insert the DOS startup disk into drive A and the *Student Resource Disk* into drive B.
2. If your instructor approves, press Ctrl-PrtScr to turn on printing.
3. Change the date to January 2, 1993.
4. Change the time to 10:30 a.m.
5. Display the path if your system has one.
6. Clear the screen.
7. Use the CHKDSK command to check the disk in drive A.

8. Display a directory of the disk in drive A in five columns.

EXERCISE 3

EXPLORING DOS 5'S DOSKEY FEATURE

In this exercise, you explore DOS 5's DOSKEY feature that allows you to repeat or edit previous commands. For this feature to work, the DOSKEY program must be loaded into memory.

1. Insert your disks as follows:
   - On a hard disk system, insert the *Student Resource Disk* into drive A.
   - On a floppy disk system, insert the DOS startup disk into drive A and the *Student Resource Disk* into drive B.
2. Enter the following command:
   - On a hard disk system, type **DIR A:** and press [Enter ←].
   - On a floppy disk system, type **DIR B:** and press [Enter ←].
3. Press [↑] to see if it displays the previous command on the command line. If so, your DOSKEY program has been loaded. If the previous command does not appear on the command line, DOSKEY has not been loaded. To load it, type **DOSKEY** and press [Enter ←]. (Immediately after it loads, a message reads *DOSKey installed*. If this message doesn't appear, ask your instructor for help.)
4. If DOSKEY is operating correctly on your system, repeat Exercise 1. Then repeat it again, but this time press [↑] until any command you want is displayed on the command line (once you have scrolled up, you can also press [↓] to back down through commands), and press [Enter ←] to execute it.
5. You can edit previous commands. To see how this works, display a previous command, and press [←] and [→] to move the cursor through it. Type new characters, and then press [Ins] and type some more. Before you press [Ins], characters you type replace any character in the cursor's position. After pressing it, new characters are inserted and text to the right is pushed aside. Use [Del] and [← Bksp] to delete characters. To cancel the command without executing it, press [Ctrl]-[C].

EXERCISE 4

LOCATING DOS FILES NEEDED FOR EXTERNAL COMMANDS

When you execute an external command, the DOS file for that command must be on a disk in one of the disk drives. If you are working on a floppy disk system that has more than one DOS disk, locate the disks that contain the files listed in the table "DOS External Command Files." The files will have the name shown in the table, but their extensions may be either .EXE or .COM. To locate the files, put each DOS disk into drive A one at a time, type **DIR A:** and press [Enter ←] to list the files on the disk. If the filenames scroll by too fast to read, type **DIR A:/W** and press [Enter ←].

DOS EXTERNAL COMMAND FILES

File	Disk
CHKDSK	_____
COMP	_____
DOSKEY	_____
FORMAT	_____
LABEL	_____
MORE	_____
PRINT	_____
SORT	_____
SYS	_____
TREE	_____
TYPE	_____
XCOPY	_____

Changing the Default Drive

After completing this topic, you will be able to:

■ Describe the difference between the default drive and other drives
■ Change default drives
■ Customize the command prompt

When you first turn on your computer to boot the system, drive A spins. If a disk in that drive contains the necessary operating system files, the operating system is loaded. Drive A operates because the computer's designers have placed a program in the computer's ROM telling it that it should address this drive when first turned on. Since it addresses drive A automatically, drive A is the default startup drive. (On a hard disk system, it then looks to drive C if no disk is in drive A.)

Although you cannot change the default drive that the computer addresses when you first turn it on, you can, and often do, copy, rename, delete, and save files on a drive other than the default drive. To do so, you can change the default drive.

The Default Drive

The default drive is the drive your computer automatically addresses when you execute commands. It's like a model railroad where you can set a switch to send a train down one track or another.

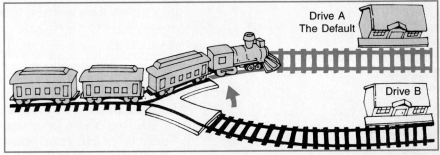

Changing the Default Drive

You can change the default drive so that the program automatically addresses another drive. It's like changing the position of the switch on a model railroad to send the train down another track.

In this tutorial, you change the default drive.

GETTING STARTED

1. Load DOS so that the command prompt is displayed.
2. Insert your disks as follows:
   - On a hard disk system, insert the *Student Resource Disk* into drive A.
   - On a floppy disk system, insert the DOS disk into drive A and the *Student Resource Disk* into drive B.

CHANGING THE COMMAND PROMPT

3. Type **PROMPT What can I do for you?** and press ⟨Enter ←⟩ to change the prompt. Changes in the prompt stay in effect until you turn off the computer unless you use the PROMPT command again to change it.
4. Type **PROMPT PG** and press ⟨Enter ←⟩. The PG at the end of the text is a DOS command that tells the computer to display the current default drive, in this case, *C:\>* or *A:\>*.
5. Type **PROMPT The default drive is now PG** and press ⟨Enter ←⟩ to have the prompt indicate the current default drive as you complete the steps that follow.

CHANGING THE DEFAULT DRIVE

6. Enter the command as follows:
   - On a hard disk system, type **C:** and press ⟨Enter ←⟩.
   - On a floppy disk system, type **B:** and press ⟨Enter ←⟩.

   When you enter this command, the command prompt changes to indicate the current default drive.
7. Type **DIR** and press ⟨Enter ←⟩ to display a list of files on the current default drive.
8. Type **A:** and press ⟨Enter ←⟩ to change the default drive to A.
9. Type **DIR** and press ⟨Enter ←⟩ to display a list of files on the new default drive.
10. Enter the command as follows:
    - On a hard disk system, type **C:** and press ⟨Enter ←⟩.
    - On a floppy disk system, type **B:** and press ⟨Enter ←⟩.
11. Type **A:** and press ⟨Enter ←⟩.

FINISHING UP

12. Type **PROMPT PG** and press ⟨Enter ←⟩ to have the prompt indicate the default drive without the preceding text.
13. Either continue to the next activity or quit for the day. To quit, remove your disks from the drives and turn off the computer.

When working with DOS and application programs, you need to change the default drive. At times, it is helpful to customize the command prompt so that it provides you with information that you need.

Changing the Default Drive

To change the default drive from the command prompt, type the letter of the drive and a colon and press (Enter←). For example, if the default drive is set to A and you want to change it to B, type **B:** and press (Enter←). The command prompt is usually set to indicate the current default drive. For example, *B>* or *B:\>* indicates that drive B is the default drive.

In a system with a single floppy disk drive, the drive functions as both drive A and drive B. If the command prompt reads *A>* and you type **B:** and press (Enter←), the command prompt changes to *B>*. On such systems, when you execute DOS commands such as copying files from one disk to another, you are frequently asked to swap disks in the drive.

Changing the Command Prompt

The default command prompt (which you get if you type **PROMPT** and press (Enter←)) is the letter of the current default drive followed by a greater-than sign, but you can customize the prompt to display other useful information. To change the command prompt, you can use any of the commands, either alone or in combination, described in the table "Prompt Commands." Note that each of these commands is preceded by a dollar sign so that it will not be treated as text and appear just as typed. The prompt command **PROMPT PG** is probably the most frequently used version. It displays the current drive (and directory, as you will see later).

PROMPT COMMANDS

Character	Description
$_	Inserts a carriage return and line feed when you want to create two or more lines on the prompt; for example, **PROMPT TIME = T_DATE = D_PG** displays the time on one line, the date on the next, and the current drive and directory on the third.
$B	Displays a I (split vertical bar).
$D	Displays the current date.
$E	Displays an ← (Esc) character.
$G	Displays a > (greater-than) character.
$H	Backspace that deletes the previous character in the prompt.
$L	Displays a < (less-than) character.
$N	Displays the default drive.
$P	Displays the current directory of the default drive. (If you use this character on a floppy disk system, the disk drive must always have a disk in it when you make it the default drive; otherwise, you get the error message *Not ready reading drive x*. (The *x* is the specified drive and varies depending on the system you are using.) If this prompt appears, press (F) (for *Fail*) to continue.
$Q	Displays an equal sign (=).

Character	Description
$T	Displays the current time.
$V	Displays the DOS version number.
$<spaces>	Type **$** and then press Spacebar to insert spaces. If you insert a space after the last character in the PROMPT command, the cursor will be spaced one character to the right of the prompt.

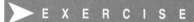

E X E R C I S E

EXERCISE 1

CHANGING BETWEEN DRIVES A AND B ON A SYSTEM WITH A SINGLE FLOPPY DISK DRIVE

If your system has only a single floppy disk drive, you can explore how it acts as both drive A and drive B. You will find this feature very useful when you want to copy files between disks in later tutorials and in your own work. As you complete the following steps, watch the prompts that appear on the screen; then press Enter↵ to remove them before proceeding to the next step. Whenever you see the prompt asking you to insert a disk, you can remove one disk and then insert another before continuing. This way you can use the single drive in your system as though it were two separate drives.

1. Load DOS.
2. Insert your *Student Resource Disk* into drive A.
3. Type **A:** and press Enter↵ so that the command prompt *A>* or *A:\>* is displayed.
4. Type **B:** and press Enter↵.
5. Type **A:** and press Enter↵.
6. Type **DIR B:** and press Enter↵.
7. Type **DIR A:** and press Enter↵.

REVIEW

- Loading the operating system is called booting the system. If the computer is off, it is called a cold boot. If the system is already on, it is called a warm boot.
- When you load DOS, either the command prompt or the DOS Shell is displayed, depending on which version of DOS you're using and how your system has been set up.
- DOS has internal and external commands. The internal commands are part of the COMMAND.COM file and are always available whenever the command prompt is displayed on the screen. External commands are stored in their own files. To use one of them, the file must be on a disk in one of the drives.
- The default drive is the drive that the computer addresses unless you specify another drive. To change the default drive, you type its letter and a colon and press Enter↵.

QUESTIONS

FILL IN THE BLANK

1. If you make a typo when typing a command, you can press _____ to delete it.

2. After typing a command, you press _____ to send it to the CPU.

3. The *A>*, *A:\>*, *C>*, *C:\>* or something similar that appears on the screen when you boot your system is called the _____ _____.

4. To enter the date January 10, 1994, into a computer, you would type _____.

5. To enter the time ten-thirty a.m. into a computer, you would type _____.

6. To warm-boot many computers, you hold down _____ and _____ and then press _____.

7. To find out what version of DOS is in your computer's memory, you use the _____ command.

8. Commands that are always available when the command prompt is on the screen are called _____ commands.

9. Commands that are available only when the file that contains them is on a disk in one of the disk drives are called _____ commands.

10. To repeat the previous command, you press _____ and then press _____.

11. To print the text currently on the screen, you would press _____.

12. To print all text that will appear on the screen with subsequent commands, you would press _____.

13. To change the way the command prompt looks, you use the _____ command.

14. To change the default drive from drive A to drive B, you type _____ and press _____.

15. To change the default drive from drive B to drive A, you type _____ and press _____.

MATCH THE COLUMNS

1. VER
2. [F3]
3. [Ctrl]-[Alt]-[Del]
4. [← Bksp]
5. Prompts
6. [⇧ Shift]-[PrtScr] or [PrtScr]
7. [Ctrl]-[PrtScr]
8. PROMPT
9. A> or A:\>
10. **A:** and then [Enter ←]
11. **B:** and then [Enter ←]

___ Repeats the previous command

___ Command prompt

___ Command that customizes the command prompt

___ Changes the default drive to drive A

___ Computer's request for you to type something

___ Prints all screen text until you turn it off

___ Prints text currently on the screen

___ Deletes typos when entering commands

___ Keys you press to warm-boot many computers

___ Changes the default drive to drive B

___ The command that tells you what version of DOS is in memory

WRITE OUT THE ANSWER

1. What does booting a computer mean?
2. What is the startup drive? Which drive is it on a floppy disk system? On a hard disk system?
3. What is the difference between a warm boot and a cold boot? How do you do each?
4. What is the basic difference between an internal and an external DOS command?
5. Name and describe the use of three function keys that can be used with DOS.
6. What is the default drive? Describe how you change it.
7. What does the *A>* prompt mean? The *B>* prompt?

CHAPTER 2

PROJECTS

PROJECT 1

VIEWING A VIDEO

Many videocassettes have been developed to introduce users to specific operating systems. Visit your library, learning center, and computer lab to see if any are available for you to view. If there are, view one, and then summarize its key points.

PROJECT 2

CREATING A DOS REFERENCE CARD

The table "Summary of DOS Commands" lists some of the most frequently used DOS command procedures. Complete the table by entering in the Command column the command you would use to perform each of the tasks. In the Type column, indicate if the command is an internal or external command.

SUMMARY OF DOS COMMANDS

Description	Command	Type
Basic Commands		
Displays DOS version number	_____	_____
Displays system date	_____	_____
Displays system time	_____	_____
Changes the command prompt	_____	_____
Clears the screen	_____	_____
Changing Default Drives		
Makes drive A the default drive	_____	_____
Makes drive B the default drive	_____	_____
Makes drive C the default drive	_____	_____

Basic DOS Utilities

Formatting Disks

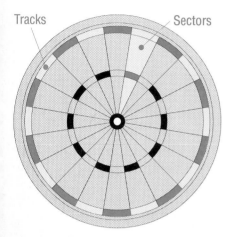

A Formatted Disk

One way to visualize a formatted disk is as a dart board. Tracks run in circles around the disk. The number of tracks per inch determines the density of the disk. A high-density disk has more tracks per inch than a low-density disk and can therefore store more data. Since the tracks can store a great deal of data, the computer divides them into sectors, which makes it easier to find a location on the disk. These sectors are like pie-shaped wedges that radiate from the center of the disk.

After completing this topic, you will be able to:

- Describe why you format a disk and what happens when you do
- Format your own data disks
- Explain the difference between a data disk and a system disk
- Format a disk as a system disk
- Transfer the operating system files to a disk that has already been formatted

When you open a box of new floppy disks, they will usually not work properly on your computer because they have been designed to work with a variety of computer systems. To customize them so that they will work with the equipment you are using, you format the disks. Formatting checks the disk surface for unusable spots, divides the disk into tracks and sectors, and creates a directory.

Formatting a disk effectively erases any data that may already have been saved on it. You therefore have to be careful with this command. You should never format a previously used disk unless you are sure you will not need any of the files on it. Moreover, you should never format a hard disk drive unless you are willing to lose every file on the disk. However, since no one is perfect and mistakes do happen, DOS 5 added an unformat command that helps you recover files should you format a disk by mistake.

▶ TUTORIALS

(your name)

Resource Disk—Backup

Formatted with DOS (version number)

The Resource Disk—Backup Label

In this tutorial, you format a blank data disk for use in the tutorials and exercises in this text.

GETTING STARTED

1. Load DOS so that the command prompt is displayed.
2. Label a blank disk, using as a guide the information shown in the figure "The Resource Disk—Backup Label."
3. Insert your disks as follows:
   - On a hard disk system, insert the disk labeled *Resource Disk—*

Backup into drive A.

- On a floppy disk system, insert the DOS disk that contains the file FORMAT.COM into drive A and the disk labeled *Resource Disk—Backup* into drive B.

4. Set your drives as follows:
   - On a hard disk system, change the default drive to drive C.
   - On a floppy disk system, change the default drive to drive A.

FORMATTING A DATA DISK

5. Enter the command as follows:
   - On a hard disk system, type **FORMAT A:** and press [Enter←].
   - On a floppy disk system, type **FORMAT B:** and press [Enter←].

   In a moment, a prompt asks you to insert a disk into the drive you entered in the FORMAT command and press or strike [Enter←] when ready. You already inserted the disks in Step 3.

6. Press [Enter←] and the drive spins as it formats the disk.
   - On DOS 4 and later versions, a message is displayed on the screen to keep you posted on the progress. When the message reads *Format complete*, the drive stops.
   - If you are using DOS 4 or later, you are prompted to enter a volume label. Type your last name (abbreviate to 11 characters if necessary), and press [Enter←] to continue.

7. When the prompt reads *Format another (Y/N)?*, press [N] and then [Enter←].

   Information is displayed on the screen about the disk's status. The information varies slightly between DOS 3 and later versions but includes the following:
   - The number of bytes of total disk space and how many bytes are currently available. Usually the two numbers are the same; if they are different, DOS may have found bad sectors on the disk. If it did, it marked them so that no data can be stored on them.
   - The number of bytes in each allocation unit and the number of allocation units are displayed on DOS 4 and later versions.
   - The volume's serial number is displayed on DOS 4 and later versions.

FINISHING UP

8. You have now completed this tutorial. Either continue to the next activity or quit for the day.

QUICK REFERENCE

To format a data disk, you use the FORMAT command. The FORMAT.COM file must be on one of the drives since this is an external command.

DOS always formats a disk to match the drive it is being formatted in unless you specify otherwise. To change the way a disk is formatted, you add switches to the FORMAT command to control the formatting process. For example, you may want to format a 360KB disk in a 1.2MB drive or a 720KB 3½-inch disk in a 1.44MB drive. To format a 360KB disk in a 1.2MB 5¼-inch drive, use the command FORMAT <*drive:*> / 4. To format a 720KB disk in a 1.44MB 3½-inch drive, use the command FORMAT <*drive:*> /T:80 /N:9 (or FORMAT <*drive:*> /F:720 on versions 4.0 and later).

➡ **K E Y / S t r o k e s**

Formatting Floppy Disks

1. Insert your disks as follows:
   - On a hard disk system, insert the disk to be formatted into drive A.
   - On a floppy disk system, insert the disk with the file FORMAT.COM into drive A and the disk to be formatted into drive B.

2. Set your drives as follows:
   - On a hard disk system, make drive C the default drive.
   - On a floppy disk system, make drive A the default drive.

3. Enter the command as follows:
   - On a hard disk system, type **FORMAT A:** and press [Enter←].
   - On a floppy disk system, type **FORMAT B:** and press [Enter←].

   In a moment, a prompt asks you to insert a disk into the drive you entered in the FORMAT command and press or strike [Enter←] when ready. You inserted the disks in Step 1.

4. Press [Enter←] to continue and the drive spins as it formats the disk. On DOS 4 and later versions, a message is displayed on the screen to keep you posted on the progress. (DOS 5 also saves UNFORMAT information.) When the message reads *Format complete*, the drive stops.

   If you are using DOS 4 or later, a prompt reads *Volume label (11 characters, ENTER for none)?*. Either type a volume name to identify the disk and press [Enter←] or press [Enter←] without entering a volume name.

   The prompt reads *Format another (Y/N)?*.

5. Either: Press [N] and then [Enter←] to quit formatting and return to the command prompt.

   Or: Insert a new disk into the same drive as you did in Step 1, press [Y] and then [Enter←] to display the prompt asking you to insert a new disk. Press the designated key to continue.

Creating System Disks

When you boot the computer, it looks in the startup drive for the file COMMAND.COM and two hidden system files named IBMBIO.COM and IBMDOS.COM (or something similar on some versions of DOS). The DOS startup disk contains these files, but you can also put them onto your own floppy disks, which are then called system disks because they can be used to boot the system.

There are two ways to transfer these files to your own floppy disk: either during or after formatting.

- To transfer the files during formatting, add the /S switch to the FORMAT command. For example, to format a disk on drive A as a system disk, type **FORMAT A: /S** and press (Enter↵). On most systems this switch copies the two hidden system system files and the file COMMAND.COM to the floppy disk. On some systems, however, it does not copy COMMAND.COM and you must copy it separately with the COPY command. (See the box "Copying COMMAND.COM.")
- If there is room for them on an already formatted floppy disk, you can transfer the two hidden system files to it with the external command SYS. For example, to transfer the system files to an already formatted disk in drive A, type **SYS A:** and press (Enter↵). The SYS command does not copy the file COMMAND.COM. You have to copy it separately with the COPY command. (See the box "Copying COMMAND.COM.")

Unformatting a Disk

If you format a disk by mistake, you can lose valuable files because the FORMAT command erases them. For this reason, many companies have published special programs you can use to restore deleted files. With the introduction of DOS 5, an UNFORMAT external command was added so that you can use DOS to unformat a disk and restore the lost files. To unformat a disk, type **UNFORMAT** *<drive>* and press (Enter↵). For example, to unformat a disk in drive A, type **UNFORMAT A:** and press (Enter↵).

To ensure that this command works, you should load DOS 5's Mirror program before formatting a disk. This program saves data that can be used to unformat the disk (specifically the file allocation table and the root directory) in a file named MIRROR.FIL. To load the Mirror program, type **MIRROR** *<drive>* and press (Enter↵). To mirror more than one drive, list each drive after the command. For example, to mirror drives A and C, type **MIRROR A: C:** and press (Enter↵). The UNFORMAT command may work on a disk that was formatted without MIRROR loaded, but your risks of not being successful increase, and the process takes longer. Moreover, for the most likelihood of success, unformat the disk immediately. If you save any files on it, they may overwrite files from the previous format, and the overwritten files will not be recoverable.

Selecting Floppy Disks for Your System

When you format a disk, the operating system divides it into tracks and sectors, an invisible magnetic pattern something like a dart board. On a formatted disk, tracks run in circles around the disk. Because tracks can store a great deal of data, the computer needs to divide them into sectors, which makes it easier to find a location on the disk. These sectors are like pie-shaped wedges that divide each track into the same number of sectors.

On early computers, disks were single-sided. All disks used now are double-sided. To store more data, the tracks on the disk are placed closer together. The spacing of these tracks is measured as tracks per inch (TPI). The number of TPI determines the density of the disk and the amount of data that can be stored on it. A high-density disk has more

---

LOOKING AHEAD: COPYING COMMAND.COM

You will learn about copying files in Topic 11. For now, just follow these directions to copy COMMAND.COM to a floppy disk.

1. Insert the DOS startup disk into drive A.
2. Insert the formatted system disk into drive B.
3. Make drive A the default drive by typing **A:** and pressing (Enter↵).
4. Type **COPY COMMAND. COM B:** and press (Enter↵).

tracks per inch than a low-density disk and can therefore store more data. The maximum density that can be used to store data on a disk is indicated on the disk label and box. For example, on 5¼-inch disks:

- Double-density disks can store data on 48 TPI or up to 360KB.
- High-density disks (also called high-capacity or quad-density disks) can store data on 96 TPI or up to 1.2MB.

The smaller 3½-inch floppy disks can store 720KB or 1.44MB. These disks can store more data than the larger 5¼-inch disks because they can store data on 135 TPI. You can tell the two types of disks apart as follows:

- A 720KB disk is labeled 1.0MB or 2HC and has a single square cutout.
- A 1.44MB disk is labeled 2.0MB or HD and has two square cutouts.

Because of these variations in the way computers assign tracks and sectors, the disks you use must be appropriate for your system. Some of the possible combinations are shown in the tables "Formatting and Reading 5¼-Inch Disks" and "Formatting and Reading 3½-Inch Disks."

Volume Labels

It can be useful to give your disks a label (name) that will appear on the screen whenever you look at their directory or use the VOL command. When you format a disk, DOS 4 and later versions automatically prompt you to enter a volume label. On earlier versions, you can add a label by using the command **FORMAT B: /V**. You can also add or change a label after a disk has been formatted with the LABEL command (an external command).

FORMATTING AND READING 5¼-INCH DISKS

Procedure	360KB Drive	1.2MB Drive
Format a 360KB disk	Yes	Yes*
Format a 1.2MB disk	No	Yes
Read a 360KB disk	Yes	Yes
Read a 1.2MB disk	No	Yes

With switches

FORMATTING AND READING 3½-INCH DISKS

Procedure	720KB Drive	1.44MB Drive
Format a 720KB disk	Yes	Yes*
Format a 1.44MB disk	No	Yes
Read a 720KB disk	Yes	Yes
Read a 1.44MB disk	No	Yes

With switches

➡ **K E Y / S t r o k e s**

Labeling a Formatted Disk

1. Insert your disks as follows:
   - On a hard disk system, make drive C the default drive.
   - On a floppy disk system, insert the disk with the LABEL.COM or LABEL.EXE file into drive A and the disk to be labeled into drive B. Make drive A the default drive.
2. Enter a command as follows:
   - On a hard disk system, type **LABEL A:** and press [Enter←].
   - On a floppy disk system, type **LABEL B:** and press [Enter←].
   A prompt reads *Volume label (11 characters, ENTER for none)?*.
3. Type a new label, and press [Enter←].

EXERCISE 1

FORMATTING ADDITIONAL DATA DISKS

Format any additional data disks that you might need for your own work.

EXERCISE 2

ADDING A VOLUME NAME

If you are using a version of DOS earlier than DOS 4, you were not prompted to enter a volume label when you formatted the *Resource Disk—Backup* in the tutorial. Use the LABEL command to label this disk with your last name (if necessary, abbreviate to 11 characters).

EXERCISE 3

CHECKING VOLUME NAMES

Use the VOL command to display the volume names for each of your floppy disks. If you find any disk with a name, write it down.

EXERCISE 4

SPECIFYING YOUR SYSTEM'S DISKS

List the specifications for the disks your system requires in the table "Disk Specifications." You will find this information in the manual that accompanies the computer. Look up "disks" or "disk drives" in the index, and refer to the listed sections. If you cannot find the information in the manual, refer to the specifications printed on the box that your disks came in.

DISK SPECIFICATIONS

Specification	Your System's Disks
Size	_____
Sides	_____
Density	_____
TPI	_____

Assigning and Listing Filenames

The file's name can have up to eight characters

The file's extension must begin with a period and can have up to three characters

Filenames
Filenames have two parts: the file's name and an optional three-character extension separated from the file's name with a period.

Character	Example
Letters	A - Z
Letters	a - z
Numbers	0 - 9
Underscore	_
Caret	^
Dollar sign	$
Tilde	~
Exclamation point	!
Number sign	#
Percent sign	%
Ampersand	&
Hyphen	-
Braces	{ }
Parentheses	( )
At sign	@
Grave accent	`
Apostrophe	'

Legal Filename Characters
You can use any of the characters shown here in your files' names and extensions. You can type filenames in uppercase letters, lowercase letters, or a combination of uppercase and lowercase. If you enter lowercase letters, the computer automatically converts them to uppercase.

After completing this topic, you will be able to:
- Describe the number and types of the characters that you can use when naming files
- List the names of files on a disk
- Use switches to modify a basic command
- Describe the function of the question mark and asterisk wildcards
- Use wildcards to specify files in commands

The files for the application programs you use have already been assigned names. When you use these programs to create and save your own work, you must assign names to your files. With DOS, you can assign names to files that have up to eight characters and an optional extension of up to three characters separated from the name by a period.

File Names
The characters that you can use in a filename are called *legal characters* and are shown in the figure "Legal Filename Characters." Using any other character results in a name the computer will not accept.

Each filename you use must be unique. If you assign a file the same name and extension as a file that is already on the disk, the new file will overwrite the previous file and erase it. However, you can use the same name with different extensions—for example, LETTER.DOC and LETTER.BAK. You can also use the same extension with different names.

Filename Extensions
Many application programs automatically enter extensions that identify files that they create. For example, Lotus 1-2-3 adds extensions such as .WK1 or .PIC to files it creates. dBASE adds extensions such as .DBF and .NDX. Conventions also dictate that some extensions are to be used only in specific situations. For instance, .EXE and .COM are normally used for program files, and .BAT is used for batch files. The extension .SYS is used for files containing information about your system's hardware. In many cases, if you don't use the extension the program automatically adds, the program will not be able to identify the file as its own. This can cause problems when you want to retrieve a file later.

Listing Files
Since a disk can hold many files, it is often necessary to find out what files are on a particular disk. The names of the files on a disk are held

in a directory, which you display with the DIR command. When you use this command, you control which files are listed and how they are listed using wildcards and switches. A wildcard is simply a character that stands for one or more other characters, much like a wildcard in a card game. DOS wildcards are the question mark (?) and the asterisk (*). A switch is an add-on to a command that modifies the command's performance. For example, you can use a switch to list filenames across the screen instead of down it, or to sort the listing by name, extension, date, or size.

▶ T U T O R I A L

In this tutorial, you list filenames with the DIR command and explore both wildcards and switches. Study carefully how wildcards are used. Although you are introduced to wildcards in this tutorial on the DIR command, keep in mind that they can be used with many DOS commands and with many application programs.

GETTING STARTED

1. Load DOS so that the command prompt is displayed.
2. Insert your disks as follows:
   - On a hard disk system, insert the *Student Resource Disk* into drive A.
   - On a floppy disk system, insert the DOS disk into drive A and the *Student Resource Disk* into drive B.
3. Set your drives as follows:
   - On a hard disk system, make drive A the default drive.
   - On a floppy disk system, make drive B the default drive.
4. Type **CD\DOS** and press [Enter←] to move to the DOS directory.

DISPLAYING A LIST OF FILENAMES

```
 Volume in drive A has no label
 Directory of A:\DOS

 .            <DIR>      05-27-92    7:39p
 ..           <DIR>      05-27-92    7:39p
 ERASE    TXT       27   01-08-92   10:23a
 ASCII    TXT     1407   03-03-89   12:19p
 BANKLOAN PRN     3318   03-03-89   10:26a
 BANKLOAN WK1     1672   01-07-92    3:00p
 CHPT1    WP5       66   01-06-92    3:07p
 CHPT2    WP5       66   01-06-92    3:07p
 CHPT3    WP5       66   01-06-92    3:07p
 CHPT4    WP5       66   01-06-92    3:07p
 CHPT5    WP5       66   01-06-92    3:07p
 FILE     TXT       18   01-01-80    1:36a
 FILE1    TXT       17   02-20-89    1:45a
 FILE10   TXT       18   01-30-91    1:49a
 FILE11   TXT       18   01-30-91    1:50a
 FILE2    TXT       17   02-20-89    1:46a
 FILE3    TXT       17   02-20-89    1:47a
 FILE4    TXT       17   02-20-89    1:47a
 FILE5    TXT       17   02-20-89    1:47a
 FILE6    TXT       17   01-30-91    1:48a
 FILE7    TXT       17   01-30-91    1:49a
 FILE8    TXT       17   01-30-91    1:49a
 FILE9    TXT       17   01-30-91    1:49a
 GIVEUP1  HUH     1108   09-10-89    8:00a
 GIVEUP2  HUH      973   09-10-89    8:01a
 README   BAT       31   03-06-89   11:28a
 README   TXT     1174   03-06-89   11:29a
 JUMPSTRT BAT       17   01-03-92    8:59a
 WHATSUP  DOC     2801   04-24-92    4:11p
        29 file(s)       13065 bytes
                       1229824 bytes free
```

A Directory Displayed from the Command Prompt

Besides listing a file's name and extension, the DIR command displays the volume name, the size of each file in bytes, the date and time the file was last saved, the number of files on the disk, and how much free space is left on the disk. (Your list will be slightly different than the one shown here).

5. Type **DIR** and press [Enter←] to list all the files in the DOS directory on the *Student Resource Disk*.
6. List the files on the disk in another drive as follows:
   - On a hard disk system, type **DIR C:** and press [Enter←].
   - On a floppy disk system, type **DIR A:** and press [Enter←].

   Note how the periods between the files' names and extensions have been replaced with spaces.

USING THE /W SWITCH TO DISPLAY THE FILENAMES HORIZONTALLY

7. Type **DIR/W** and press [Enter←] to list the files on the default drive in five columns. The /W switch lists the files on the *Student Resource Disk* in five columns. To make room for the new columns of filenames, the size, date, and time have been dropped.
8. Display the files on the other drive in the same way:
   - On a hard disk system, type **DIR C:/W** and press [Enter←].
   - On a floppy disk system, type **DIR A:/W** and press [Enter←].

9. Enter a command as follows:
   - On a hard disk system, type **DIR /P** and press [Enter←].
   - On a floppy disk system, type **DIR /P** and press [Enter←].

   The /P switch displays the filenames in the DOS directory on the *Student Resource Disk* until the screen is full and then pauses and displays a prompt asking you to press or strike a key to continue. Do so, and the list continues to scroll.

USING THE * WILDCARD

10. Type **DIR** and press [Enter←] to list all the files on the default drive. (The filenames followed by *<DIR>* are subdirectories, which you will learn about later in this text.)

11. Type **DIR *.*** and press [Enter←] to list all the files on the default drive again.

12. Type **DIR F*.*** and press [Enter←] to list all files that begin with the letter F.

13. Type **DIR C*.*** and press [Enter←] to list all files that begin with the letter C.

14. Type **DIR *.TXT** and press [Enter←] to list all files with the extension *.TXT*.

15. Type **DIR *.BAK** and press [Enter←] to list all files with the extension *.BAK*.

16. Type **DIR *.DOC** and press [Enter←] to list all files with the extension *.DOC*.

USING THE ? WILDCARD

17. Type **DIR** and press [Enter←] to list all the files on the default drive again.

18. Type **DIR FILE?.TXT** and press [Enter←] to list all files that begin with *FILE*, have up to one additional character, and have the extension *.TXT*. The files with the names FILE10.TXT and FILE11.TXT are not listed.

19. Type **DIR FILE??.TXT** and press [Enter←] to list all files that begin with *FILE*, have up to two additional characters, and have the extension *.TXT*. Now the files with the names FILE10.TXT and FILE11.TXT are listed.

20. Type **DIR CHPT?.???** and press [Enter←] to list all files that begin with *CHPT*, have up to one additional character, and have any extension.

21. Type **DIR C*.???** and press [Enter←] to list all files beginning with *C* and with any extension of three or fewer characters.

22. Type **DIR ?????.*** and press [Enter←] to list all filenames with five or fewer characters and any extension.

23. Type **DIR F??E?.*** and press [Enter←] to list all filenames with four or five characters that begin with F and have E as its fourth character and any extension.

24. Press [F3] and then [Enter←] to repeat the previous command.

SORTING THE DIR LISTING

25. To list files in alphabetical order by name, enter a command as follows:
    - If you are using DOS 4 or earlier, type **DIR | SORT** and press [Enter←].
    - If you are using DOS 5 or later, type **DIR /ON** and press [Enter←].

    SORT is an external command, so if you use that command and a message tells you that it is a bad command or filename, the SORT.EXE file is not on the disk you are using. Ask your instructor which disk contains the file.

26. To list files in alphabetical order by extension, enter a command as follows:
    - If you are using DOS 4 or earlier, type **DIR SORT /+10** and press [Enter←].
    - If you are using DOS 5 or later, type **DIR /OE** and press [Enter←].

27. To list files in order by size, enter a command as follows:
    - If you are using DOS 4 or earlier, type **DIR SORT /+14** and press [Enter←].
    - If you are using DOS 5 or later, type **DIR /OS** and press [Enter←].

28. To list files in order by date, enter a command as follows:
    - If you are using DOS 4 or earlier, type **DIR SORT /+24** and press [Enter←], to sort by the month but not the year.
    - If you are using DOS 5 or later, type **DIR /OD** and press [Enter←], to sort by the month and the year.

FINISHING UP

29. You have now completed this tutorial. Either continue to the next activity or quit for the day.

▶ Q U I C K   R E F E R E N C E

The names of files on a disk are stored in a directory that you can display with the DIR command. You can control which files are listed, and how they are listed, by adding wildcards and switches to the command.

The DIR Command
In its simplest form, the DIR command displays a listing of the directory of the disk in the default drive. For example, with the *A>* command prompt on the screen:

- To list the files in drive A, type **DIR** or **DIR A:** and press [Enter←].
- To see the files in drive B, type **DIR B:** and press [Enter←].

Besides listing filenames, the DIR command also displays the size of each file in bytes, the date and time the file was last saved, and the number of files in the current directory and the amount of free space left on the disk. DOS 5 and later versions also indicate the number of bytes occupied by the files in the current directory.

Using Switches with the DIR Command

If a list of files is too long to be displayed on the screen, some of the filenames will quickly scroll up and off the top of the screen. Two commands prevent this: DIR *<drive>* /W and DIR *<drive>* /P. The /W and /P following the commands are called switches and they modify the basic command.

With DOS 5, other switches can be used to arrange ("or sort") the list by name, extension, date, or size in ascending or descending order. All switches that can be used with the DIR command are listed and described in the table "DIR Command Switches."

DIR COMMAND SWITCHES

DOS 5 Switch	DOS 4 Switch	Description
/W	/W	The /W (for Wide) switch displays five columns of filenames instead of a single vertical list. This command drops the file size, date, and time information to make room for the additional columns of filenames. Because only the filenames are displayed and they are arranged horizontally on the screen, many filenames can be displayed on the screen at one time.
/P	/P	The /P (for Pause) switch displays filenames until the screen is full. The list then pauses, and a prompt reads *Press any key to continue*. To display more filenames, simply press any key.
/ON	ISORT	Lists file names in ascending alphabetical order.
/O-N	ISORT /R	Lists file names in descending alphabetical order.
/OE	ISORT /+10	Lists file extensions in ascending alphabetical order.
/O-E	ISORT /+10 /R	Lists file extensions in descending alphabetical order.
/OS	ISORT /+14	Lists files by size from smallest to largest.
/O-S	ISORT /+14 /R	Lists files by size from largest to smallest.
/OD	ISORT /+24	Lists files by dates from newest to oldest (DOS 4 and earlier versions sort only by month, not year.)
/O-D	ISORT /+24 /R	Lists files by dates from oldest to newest (DOS 4 and earlier versions sort only by month, not year.)

The Directory Arrangement

A directory is actually arranged into 38 columns. Each section begins in its own column, which you can specify to sort the directory by that section. For example, to sort on the extension, you specify /+10. To sort on the file's size, you specify /+14.

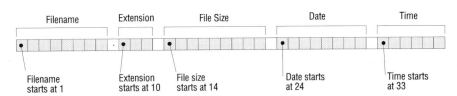

| Filename | Extension | File Size | Date | Time |
| Filename starts at 1 | Extension starts at 10 | File size starts at 14 | Date starts at 24 | Time starts at 33 |

On DOS 4 and earlier versions, sorting directories is more complicated. First of all, you cannot use a sort switch with the DIR command directly. Instead, you have to use the pipe character [|] (the split vertical bar above the [\]) with the SORT command and add a switch to that command as shown in the table. You then have to use a second switch to sort directories in reverse order. If you look at a directory listing carefully (see the figure "The Directory Arrangement"), you will see that each element, be it name, extension, size, or date, begins in a specific column. The numbers in the switches are the columns in which the first character of the element appears in the directory. For example, the file

Wildcards

The term *wildcard* comes from card games where a designated card, say a jack, can substitute for any other card in the deck. For example, in the card sequence 4-5-J-7-8, the jack stands for the 6 card.

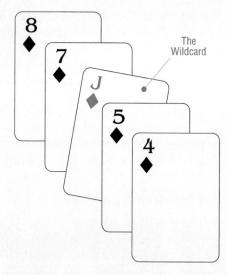

The Wildcard

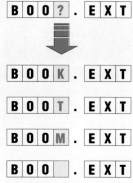

The Question Mark Wildcard

In this figure, the question mark will substitute for any character in the fourth and last position in the file's name. All other characters in filenames must be exactly as shown for a match to occur. This filename specification will therefore match files with names such as BOOK.EXT, BOOT.EXT, BOOM.EXT, and BOO.EXT.

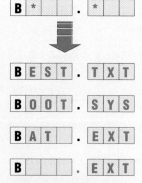

The Asterisk Wildcard

In this figure, the asterisk will substitute for all characters following the first character in the file's name and all characters in the extension. This filename specification will therefore match files beginning with the letter B that have up to eight characters in their name and any extension.

extensions are listed in the directory beginning in column 10, sizes in column 14, and dates in column 24.

Using Wildcards with the DIR Command

You use the ? and * wildcards to specify groups of files.

Using the ? Wildcard

The question mark substitutes for any single character. If you think of all filenames fitting into a grid with eight columns for the name and three columns for the extension, you can see how the question mark wildcard works.

- **????????.???** stands for the names of all files on the disk.
- **BOO?.EXT** stands for any name that has three or four characters and that begins with BOO followed by the extension .EXT.
- **BO??.EXT** stands for any name that has two to four characters and that begins with BO followed by the extension .EXT.
- **B???.???** stands for any name that has one to four characters and that begins with B followed by any extension of three or fewer characters.
- **????.E??** stands for any name that has four or fewer characters followed by any extension that begins with E.

Using the * Wildcard

The asterisk represents any character in a given position and all following characters in the part of the filename (either the name or extension) where it is used. For example, to display all filenames with the extension .DOC, type **DIR *.DOC**. Again, if you think of all filenames fitting into a grid with eight columns for the name and three columns for the extension, you can see how the asterisk wildcard works.

- ***.*** stands for any name and any extension.
- **B*.*** stands for any name that begins with B and has any extension.
- **B*.EXE** stands for any name that begins with B and has an .EXE extension.
- ***.E*** stands for any name that has an extension that begins with E.

EXERCISE 1

PRINTING DIRECTORIES

1. Turn on your printer.
2. If your instructor approves, press [Ctrl]-[PrtScr] to turn on printing.
3. Insert the *Student Resource Disk* into a floppy drive and make that drive the default drive.
4. Type **CD\DOS** and press [Enter←] to change to the DOS directory.
5. Display filenames on your original *Student Resource Disk* so that names, extensions, sizes and dates are listed.
6. Display filenames on your original *Student Resource Disk* so that just the filenames are listed in five columns.
7. Turn off printing if you turned it on.

STUDENT RESOURCE DISK FILENAME EXTENSIONS

Extension	Number
BAK	_____
BAT	_____
DOC	_____
HUH	_____
PRN	_____
TXT	_____
WK1	_____
WP5	_____

EXERCISE 2

USING WILDCARDS

1. Insert the *Student Resource Disk* into drive A and make that the default drive. Then type **CD\DOS** and press [Enter←] to change to the DOS directory.
2. Using the *.<ext> filename specifications, list in the table "Student Resource Disk Filename Extensions" the number of files there are with each extension. For example, to complete the first entry, type **DIR *.BAK** and press [Enter←]. Then list in the table the number of filenames displayed.

Copying Files

- Describe the difference between the source and target drives
- Copy files from one disk to another

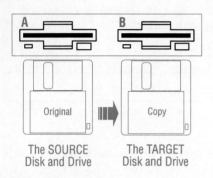

Source and Target Drives

The source drive is the one containing the files you want to copy. The target drive is the one you want them copied to.

The SOURCE Disk and Drive   The TARGET Disk and Drive

To copy files from one disk to another, you use the COPY command. This command is often used to make backup copies of important files. When you use this command, you usually must specify three things:

1. The drive containing the disk the files are to be copied from—the source drive unless it is the default drive.
2. The name of the files to be copied.
3. The drive containing the disk the files are to be copied to—the target drive unless it is the default drive.

Keep in mind that the source is the drive containing the disk that you want the action performed on. The target is the drive containing the disk that you want to be affected by the source. For example, to copy a file from drive A to drive B, you use the command COPY A:FILENAME.EXT B:. The A: specifies the source drive that contains the file to be copied, and the B: specifies the target drive that you want the file copied to.

If your system has only one floppy disk drive, specify the source drive as drive A and the target drive as drive B. The operating system will then prompt you to swap disks whenever it needs access to the source or target disk and it is not in the drive.

▶ T U T O R I A L

In this tutorial, you copy the files from your original *Student Resource Disk* to the disk labeled *Resource Disk—Backup* that you formatted in Topic 9.

GETTING STARTED

1. Load DOS so that the command prompt is displayed.
2. Insert your disks as follows:
   - On a hard disk system, insert the *Student Resource Disk* into drive A.
   - On a floppy disk system, insert the *Student Resource Disk* into drive A and the disk you labeled *Resource Disk—Backup* into drive B.
3. Make drive A the default drive.

NOTE ABOUT SINGLE FLOPPY DISK SYSTEMS

If your system has a single floppy disk drive, it will act as both drive A and drive B during this tutorial. You will be periodically prompted to swap disks during the procedure.

■ When the prompt asks you to insert a disk into drive A, insert the original *Student Resource Disk.*

■ When the prompt asks you to insert a disk into drive B, insert the *Resource Disk— Backup.*

After swapping disks, press any key to continue.

LOOKING AHEAD: XCOPY COMMAND

When you use the COPY A:*.* B: command on a single disk drive system, you have to swap disks for each and every file. To avoid this problem, use the command XCOPY A:*.* B: instead. This command is discussed in detail in Topic 16.

COPYING A SINGLE FILE

4. Type **COPY WHATSUP.DOC B:** and press ⌷Enter ←⌷. A message reads *1 file(s) copied*, and the command prompt reappears.

5. Type **DIR B:** and press ⌷Enter ←⌷ to see that the file was copied.

COPYING FILES USING A WILDCARD

6. Type **COPY C*.WP5 B:** and press ⌷Enter ←⌷ to copy all files beginning with the letter *C* and ending with the extension .WP5. As each file is copied, its name is listed on the screen.

7. Type **DIR B:** and press ⌷Enter ←⌷ to see that only those files beginning with the letter *C* and ending with the extension .WP5 were copied to drive B.

COPYING A FILE WITH THE TARGET DIRECTORY AS THE DEFAULT

8. Make drive B the default drive.

9. Type **COPY A:FILE1.TXT** and press ⌷Enter ←⌷ to copy the file FILE1.TXT from drive A to drive B.

10. Type **DIR** and press ⌷Enter ←⌷ to see that the file was copied to the disk in drive B even though that drive wasn't specified in the command.

COPYING ALL FILES

11. On a hard disk system, be sure the original *Student Resource Disk* is in drive A. (If your system has one floppy drive, see the box "Looking Ahead: XCOPY Command.")

12. Type **COPY A:*.* B:** and press ⌷Enter ←⌷ to copy all the files on drive A to the disk in drive B. As each file is copied, its name is listed on the screen.

13. Type **DIR B:** and press ⌷Enter ←⌷ to see that all files were copied. You have a duplicate of the *Student Resource Disk* (except for the subdirectories you will learn about later).

FINISHING UP

14. Either continue to the next activity or quit for the day.

▶ QUICK REFERENCE

The COPY command is an internal command that you can use to copy single files or groups of files. When using it, you must specify the source and target drives only if they are not the default drives. For example:

■ If the default drive is set to A, and you want to copy a file named LETTER on drive A to drive B, you would type **COPY LETTER B:**. This command reads "copy the file named LETTER in the default drive to drive B." You do not need to specify drive A because that is the default drive.

■ If the default drive is set to B, and you want to copy a file named LETTER on drive A to drive B, you would type **COPY A:LETTER**. The command reads "copy the file named LETTER in drive A to the

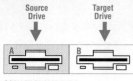

COPY FILENAME.EXT B:

COPY A:FILENAME.EXT

COPY A:FILENAME.EXT B:

Specifying Drives in Commands

Three possible copying situations are illustrated here. In the first, the source drive is the default (shown tinted), so you need to specify only the target drive in a command. In the second, the target drive is the default, so you need to specify only the source drive in a command. In the third, neither drive is the default, so you must specify both the source and target drives in a command.

default drive." You do not need to specify drive B because that is the default drive.

- Regardless of which drive is the default, you can specify both the source and target drives as a precaution. For example, to copy the file named LETTER from drive A to drive B regardless of which drive is the default drive, type **COPY A:LETTER B:**. This command reads "copy the file named LETTER in drive A to drive B."

If you copy a file to a disk or directory that already has a file by the same name, the copied file overwrites and replaces the original file.

→ **K E Y / S t r o k e s**

Copying Files

1. Insert your disks as follows:
   - On a hard disk system, insert the source disk into drive A. You will be prompted to swap disks periodically.
   - On a floppy disk system, insert the source disk into drive A and the target disk into drive B.
2. Either: Type **COPY A:*.* B:** and press Enter↵ to copy all files.
   Or: Type **COPY A:**<*filename.ext*> **B:** and press Enter↵ to copy a single file.

▶ E X E R C I S E

EXERCISE 1

COPYING FILES

1. To copy all files with the extension .DOC from drive A to drive B, you would type _____.
2. To copy all files with the extension .TXT from drive B to drive A, you would type _____.
3. To copy all files beginning with the letter A and with the extension .DOC from drive A to drive B, you would type _____
   _____.
4. To copy all files beginning with the letters CHPT followed by any single digit number (for example, CHPT1, CHPT 2, and so on) from drive A to drive B, you would type_____.

Renaming Files

> **After completing this topic, you will be able to:**
> - Rename files one at a time
> - Rename groups of files using wildcards

There are times when you want to change the name of a file on a disk. For example, you may rename them to make your filenames consistent or to free up a name so you can use it for another file.

▶ T U T O R I A L S

Renaming Files
When you rename a file, you don't affect its contents, just the name it goes by.

In this tutorial, you rename some of the files on the disk labeled *Resource Disk—Backup.* To do so, you use both the RENAME command and the shorthand version REN, which has the same effect.

GETTING STARTED

1. Load DOS so that the command prompt is displayed.
2. Insert the disk labeled *Resource Disk—Backup* into drive A, and make that the default drive.

SELECTING FILES TO BE RENAMED

3. Type **DIR CHPT *.*** and press Enter⏎ to display all files beginning with the letters CHPT.

RENAMING SINGLE FILES

4. Type **RENAME CHPT1.DOC CHPT6.WP5** and press Enter⏎ to rename the file.
5. Type **DIR *.WP5** and press Enter⏎ to see that the file is now listed under its new name, CHPT6.WP5, instead of its old name, CHPT1.DOC.

RENAMING GROUPS OF FILES USING WILDCARDS

6. Type **REN CHPT?.WP5 CHPT?.NEW** and press Enter⏎ to rename all files that begin with CHPT, have one or fewer additional letters, and end with the extension .WP5.
7. Type **DIR CHPT?.*** and press Enter⏎ to see that the files are listed under their original filenames but end with the extension .NEW instead of .WP5.

8. Type **REN CHPT?.NEW CHPT?.WP5** and press [Enter↵] to change the names back to the way they were.

9. Type **DIR CHPT?.*** and press [Enter↵] to see that the files are now listed under their original filenames.

FINISHING UP

10. Either continue to the next activity or quit for the day.

> ## Q U I C K   R E F E R E N C E

To rename files, you use the RENAME or REN command and specify both the old name and the new name for the file. You can also specify a path for the original file if it is not on the default drive. For example, to rename a file on drive A named OLDNAME.EXT to NEWNAME.EXT, you would use the command RENAME A:OLDNAME.EXT NEWNAME.EXT.

You can also use wildcards to rename groups of files. For example, to rename all files named CHPT1.WP5 through CHPT9.WP5 so that their extension becomes .DOC, you use the command REN CPTH?.WP5 CHPT?.DOC.

→ K E Y / S t r o k e s

Renaming Files

1. Select the file that you want to rename, and make the drive that it's on the default drive.

2. Type **REN** <*oldname.ext*> <*newname.ext*> and press [Enter↵].

You can also change the name of a file while copying it. For example, to copy and change the name of a file named OLDNAME.EXT, you type **COPY OLDNAME.EXT NEWNAME.EXT** and press [Enter↵].

> ## E X E R C I S E S

EXERCISE 1

RENAMING A FILE

1. Insert the disk labeled *Resource Disk—Backup* into one of the disk drives, and make that drive the default drive.

2. Use the command **REN FILE?.TXT PART?.TXT** to rename all the files that begin with FILE, have four or five characters, and end with the extension .TXT.

3. Use the DIR *.TXT command to see the results. Why were the files named FILE10.TXT and FILE11.TXT not renamed? What command would you use to change the FILE part of their name to PART?

EXERCISE 2

COPYING AND RENAMING FILES

1. Copy the file WHATSUP.DOC from the original *Student Resource Disk* to the *Resource Disk—Backup*, and change its name to MYFILE.DOC.

2. Copy the CHPT files with the extension .WP5 from and to the *Resource Disk-Backup* disk, changing their extensions to TXT as you do so. (*Hint*: You can specify the source files as CHPT?.WP5 and the target files as CHPT?.TXT to copy them in one step since they all contain five characters and only the last one varies.)

Deleting Files

After completing this topic, you will be able to:
■ Preview files that will be deleted
■ Delete files from a disk
■ Undelete files with DOS 5 and later versions

Monitoring the amount of free space on a disk is important because many application programs misbehave when you ask them to save files on a full disk. Some programs, for example, create temporary files on your disks, and they cannot do so if the disk is too full. Most people tend to keep files long after they are useful. It is good practice to occasionally use the DIR command to list the files on a disk and then delete any of them that you no longer need.

▶ TUTORIAL

In this tutorial, you delete files from the disk labeled *Resource Disk—Backup* using the ERASE and DEL commands.

GETTING STARTED

1. Load DOS so that the command prompt is displayed.
2. Insert the disk labeled *Resource Disk—Backup* into drive A, and make that the default drive.

PREVIEWING THE FILES TO BE DELETED

3. Type **DIR *.BAK** and press Enter← to display a list of files with the extension .BAK.

DELETING A SINGLE FILE

4. Type **ERASE CHPT1.BAK** and press Enter← to delete the file.
5. Type **DIR *.BAK** and press Enter← to see that the file CHPT1.BAK is no longer listed in the directory.

DELETING ALL FILES WITH THE SAME EXTENSION

6. Type **DIR *.BAK** and press Enter← to preview which files would be deleted using the *.BAK filename specification.
7. Type **DEL *.BAK** and press Enter← to delete all files with the .BAK extension.

91_SALES.WP5   91_T&E.WK1
92_SALES.WP5   92_T&E.WK1
93_SALES.WP5   93_T&E.WK1

Deleting Files
When you delete a file, you permanently remove it from the disk and can no longer use it (although you can recover it in some situations).

8. Type **DIR *.BAK** and press Enter⏎ to see that a message reads *File not found* since all files with the extension .BAK have been deleted.

9. Either continue to the next activity or quit for the day.

> ▷ Q U I C K   R E F E R E N C E

To manage your files you have to use the ERASE or DEL command to delete unneeded files. If you are using DOS 5 or later versions, you can also often recover or undelete files should you delete them by mistake.

Deleting Files

To delete one or more files, you use the ERASE or DEL command. These two internal commands are interchangeable—they work exactly alike. For example, to delete a file on drive B named FILENAME.EXT, you type either **ERASE B:FILENAME.EXT** or **DEL B:FILENAME.EXT** and press Enter⏎.

You can use wildcards with the ERASE and DEL commands, but it is dangerous to do so. Even a slight miscalculation can cause the wrong files to be deleted. However, there are precautions you can take:

■ One way to use wildcards safely is to preview what files will be affected by specifying the planned wildcards in the DIR command. If only the files you want to delete are listed, the same wildcards are safe to use with the ERASE or DEL command. For example, if you want to delete all files with the extension .BAK, type **DIR *.BAK**. If the displayed list of files can all be deleted, type **DEL *.BAK** (or type **DEL** and press F3).

■ To be prompted for each file when using DOS 4 or later, use the /P switch. For example, to delete all files with the extension .BAK, type **DEL *.BAK/P**. Before each file is deleted, a prompt reads *Delete (Y/N)?*. Press Y to delete the file, or press N to leave the file on the disk.

■ If you use the *.* wildcards, a prompt reads *Are you sure (Y/N)?*. Press Y to continue and delete all the files, or press N to cancel the command.

> → K E Y / S t r o k e s

Deleting Files from the Disk

1. Select the name of the file you want to delete, and make the drive that it's on the default drive.
2. Type **ERASE** *<filename>* or **DEL** *<filename>* and press Enter⏎ .

Undeleting Files with DOS 5

The ERASE and DEL commands do not actually delete a file from the disk. They merely change the first letter of its name so that the name no longer appears when you display the disk's directory. This also makes the space the file occupies on the disk available for overwriting by another file. If you delete a file by mistake, do not save any files on the disk because utility programs are available that you can use to restore deleted files by putting the first letter back into their filename. One such utility program, the UNDELETE command, has been included with DOS 5 and later versions.

To undelete a file, type **UNDELETE** *<filename>* and press [Enter←]. For example, to undelete a file named LETTER91.WP5 on a disk in drive A, type **UNDELETE A:/LETTER91.WP5** and press [Enter←]. You can also use wildcards to undelete groups of files. For example, to undelete all files with the extension .WK1 of drive B, type **UNDELETE A:/*.WK1** and press [Enter←]. If you are not using the Mirror program to track deletions (see below), you are prompted to enter the first character in the file's name. You can also use the /ALL switch to undelete all files. If you use this switch and are not using the Mirror program to track deletions, the number sign (#) is used as the first character in each file's name. You can then use the REN command to rename the files.

To ensure that the UNDELETE command works, you should use the command MIRROR /T*<drive>* to store data about files that have been deleted. For example, to store data that can be used to undelete files on drive A, type **MIRROR /TA** and press [Enter←]. To mirror more than one drive, list each drive after the command. For example, to mirror drives A and C, type **MIRROR /TA /TC** and press [Enter←]. The first time you delete a file after loading this program, a file named PCTRACKR.DEL is created in the root directory of the drive. This file contains data that can be used to undelete files. As you delete additional files, information about them is added to the PCTRACKR.DEL file. With deletion tracking on, you can display a list of deleted files with the /LIST switch. For example, to list all deleted files on drive A, type **UNDELETE A: /LIST** and press [Enter←].

The UNDELETE command may work without the Mirror program tracking deletions, but your risks of not being successful increase and you have to enter the first letter of each filename when prompted to do so. Moreover, for the highest degree of success, undelete the files immediately.

► E X E R C I S E S

EXERCISE 1

COPYING AND THEN DELETING FILES

1. Insert the disk labeled *Resource Disk—Backup* into one of the disk drives.
2. Copy and rename all CHPT?.WP5 files to CHPT?.BAK files.
3. Delete the CHPT?.BAK files.

EXERCISE 2

DELETING A FILE

1. Insert the disk labeled *Resource Disk—Backup* into one of the disk drives.
2. Delete the ERASE.TXT file if it is on the disk.

EXERCISE 3

UNDELETING FILES WITH DOS 5

1. Insert the disk labeled *Resource Disk—Backup* into one of the disk drives.
2. Use the /LIST switch to list all deleted files.
3. Undelete one of the files.

REVIEW

- To use a new disk on your computer, you must first format it with the FORMAT command. This is an external command.
- To specify a drive other than the default, you must enter its address in the command. To display a directory of the files on the default drive, you type **DIR** and press [Enter ←]. To display them on drive B when that is not the default drive, you type **DIR B:** and press [Enter ←].
- Filenames on DOS computers can have eight characters followed by an extension of up to three characters (separated from the filename by a period).
- To specify more than one filename in a command on DOS computers, you use wildcards. The question mark wildcard stands for any character in the position you enter it. The asterisk wildcard stands for any character in the position you enter it and all the characters that follow up to the end of either the filename or the extension.
- The command you use to list the files on a disk is DIR, which is an internal command. You can add switches to the DIR command. DIR/W displays filenames across the screen, and DIR/P displays a screenful of names and then stops.
- The command you use to copy files is COPY, an internal command. You can use wildcards to copy groups of files. For example, COPY A:*.* B: copies all files on the disk in drive A to the disk in drive B.
- The command you use to erase files is ERASE or DEL, both of which are internal commands.
- The command you use to rename a file is RENAME (or REN), which is an internal command.

QUESTIONS

FILL IN THE BLANK

1. To prepare a disk for use on your system the first time, you usually must _____ it.
2. The command you would use to format a disk on drive B is _____.
3. DOS filenames can have up to _____ characters and an optional _____-character-long extension.
4. To list the files on a disk in drive B, you would use the command _____.
5. To list the files on a disk in drive B so that the screen display pauses when it is full, you would use the command _____.
6. To list the files on a disk in drive B in five columns, you would use the command _____.

7. To list all files with the extension .DOC on a disk in drive A, you would use the command _____.

8. To list all files with the filename LETTER and any extension on a disk in drive A, you would use the command _____.

9. To sort a directory listing of drive B by filename extension, you would enter the command _____.

10. To copy a file named REPORT.WK1 from a disk in drive A to a disk in drive B when neither drive is the default, you would use the command _____.

11. To copy a file named REPORT.WK1 from a disk in drive A to a disk in drive B when drive A is the default, you would use the command _____.

12. To copy all files from a disk in drive B to a disk in drive A, you would use the command _____.

13. To change the name of a file on drive A from OLDFILE.TXT to NEWFILE.DOC, you would use the command _____.

14. To delete a file named OLD.TXT from a disk in drive A, you would use the command _____.

MATCH THE COLUMNS

1. FORMAT	__ A switch added to the DIR command to pause the screen when it is full
2. FORMAT/S	
3. DIR	__ A wildcard that stands for a single character
4. /P	
5. /W	__ Changes the name of a file
6. *	__ Command used to copy files
7. ?	__ Displays a list of files on the disk
8. COPY	__ Formats a disk as a system disk
9. COPY *.*	__ Erases specified files
10. RENAME	__ A switch added to the DIR command to display filenames in five columns
11. ERASE	
	__ A wildcard that stands for more than one character
	__ Command that copies all files
	__ Prepares a disk so that you can store data on it

WRITE OUT THE ANSWERS

1. What is the difference between a system disk and a data disk?

2. What are the two parts of a filename called? How many characters are allowed for each part? What are the parts separated with?

3. What switch do you use to display filenames horizontally across the screen? What switch do you use to display filenames one page at a time?

4. What are wildcards used for? What two wildcards are used with DOS? Describe what each does.

5. If you are using commands that erase or copy files, how can you preview the results the commands will have?

6. When the default drive is set to A, what command do you enter to copy a file named FILENAME.EXT from drive A to drive B?

7. When the default drive is set to A, what command do you enter to copy a file named FILENAME.EXT from drive B to drive A?

8. What command do you use to rename a file? Is this command internal or external?

9. Can you rename a file while copying it? If so, how?

10. What command do you use to delete files?

11. Why must you be careful when using wildcards to delete files?

12. When using wildcards to delete groups of files, how can you preview the names of the files to be deleted?

13. Can you retrieve a file that you inadvertently deleted? What should you do to salvage it?

PROJECTS

PROJECT 1

SPECIFYING COMMANDS

Assume that drive C is the default drive and your system has two floppy disk drives, A and B. Write out the commands you would use to accomplish the following procedures:

1. Format a disk in drive A.
2. List the files on a disk in drive B so that the screen pauses when full.
3. Copy a file named LETTER.91 from drive A to B.
4. Erase all files on drive A that have the extension .BAK.

PROJECT 2

CREATING A DOS REFERENCE CARD

Complete the table "Summary of DOS Commands" by entering in the Command column the command you would use to perform each of the tasks. In the Type column, indicate if the command is an internal or external command.

SUMMARY OF DOS COMMANDS

Description	Command	Type
Formatting Disks		
Formats a data disk in drive A	_____	_____
Formats a data disk and adds a volume label	_____	_____
Adds a volume label to any disk	_____	_____
Formats a system disk in drive A	_____	_____
Displaying Lists of Files		
Lists the files on drive A	_____	_____
Lists all files on drive B with a .DOC extension	_____	_____
Wildcards		
Stands for any single character	_____	_____
Stands for any group of characters	_____	_____
Copying Files		
Copies individual files	_____	_____
Copies all files from drive A to B	_____	_____
Renaming and Erasing Files		
Renames files	_____	_____
Deletes files	_____	_____

Directories & Paths

Using Directories

File Drawers

Directories are a way to organize electronic files on a disk, just as paper files are easier to work with when organized in filing cabinets.

Unorganized file drawers make it difficult to find files when you need them.

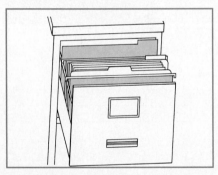

Organized file drawers make it easy to find the files you want.

After completing this topic, you will be able to:
- Explain how disks can be organized into directories and subdirectories
- Change directories
- Display lists of directories and files

Dividing a disk into directories helps you organize your files better. Imagine using a file drawer to store all of your memos, letters, and reports. Before long, the drawer would become so crowded and disorganized that you could not find anything. But with a little organization and planning, the documents could be organized into folders, making it easier to locate the one you needed.

A hard disk is like an empty drawer in a new filing cabinet: It provides a lot of storage space but no organization. To make it easier to find items in the drawer, you can divide it into categories with hanging folders. You can file documents directly into the hanging folders, or you can divide them into finer categories with manila folders. A directory is like a hanging folder, and a subdirectory is like a manila folder within a hanging folder. A file in a directory or subdirectory is like a letter, report, or other document within either a hanging folder or a manila folder.

Directories on a hard disk drive are organized in a hierarchy. The main directory, the one not below any other directory, is the root directory. Below it, directories can be created on one or more levels. These directories can hold files or subdirectories. The terms *directory* and *subdirectory* are used somewhat loosely. Strictly speaking, there is only one directory—the root directory—and all others are subdirectories. In most discussions, however, any directory above another is called a directory, and those below it are called its subdirectories.

> ### TUTORIAL

In this tutorial, you explore changing directories on the original *Student Resource Disk*.

GETTING STARTED

1. Load DOS so that the command prompt is displayed.

2. Insert your disks as follows:
   - On a hard disk system, insert the *Student Resource Disk* into drive A.
   - On a floppy disk system, insert the disk with the DOS file TREE.COM into drive A and the *Student Resource Disk* into drive B.
3. Set your drives as follows:
   - On a hard disk system, make drive A the default drive.
   - On a floppy disk system, make drive B the default drive.
4. Type **PROMPT PG** and press Enter↵ so that the prompt indicates the current drive and directory.

CHANGING THE CURRENT DIRECTORY

5. Type **DIR** and press Enter↵ to list all the files on the disk.
6. Type **DIR *.** and press Enter↵ to display just directories off the current directory. On this disk, there are four directories, each followed by *<DIR>*.
7. Type **CD\1-2-3** and press Enter↵ to make the 1-2-3 directory the current directory, and the command prompt reads *A:\1-2-3* or *B:\1-2-3*.
8. Type **DIR** and press Enter↵ to see that the 1-2-3 directory contains a subdirectory named *OLD <DIR>*. The two *<DIR>*s listed next to the periods indicate hidden files and can be ignored.

MOVING BETWEEN DIRECTORIES

9. Type **CD OLD** and press Enter↵ to move down one level, and the prompt now reads *A:\1-2-3\OLD>* or *B:\1-2-3\OLD>*. This indicates that you are in a subdirectory named OLD below the directory named 1-2-3, which is below the root directory A:\ or B:\.
10. Type **CD..** and press Enter↵ to move up one level, and the prompt now reads *A:\1-2-3>* or *B:\1-2-3>*.
11. Type **CD** and press Enter↵ to return to the root directory, and the prompt now reads *A:\>* or *B:\>*.

DISPLAYING A LIST OF DIRECTORIES AND FILES

12. Enter a command as follows:
    - On a hard disk system, type **TREE A:** and press Enter↵.
    - On a floppy disk system, type **A:TREE B:** and press Enter↵.

    A list of the directories is displayed. DOS 4 and later versions show them graphically whereas DOS 3 and earlier versions just list them.
13. Enter a command as follows:
    - On a hard disk system, type **TREE A:/F** and press Enter↵.
    - On a floppy disk system, type **A:TREE B:/F** and press Enter↵.

    Both the directories and the files on the disk are displayed. Notice how when you execute this command, the files cannot all be displayed on the screen at the same time.
14. Press F3 and then Enter↵ to repeat the command. Press Ctrl-S or Pause to pause the screen display at any point. Press any key to

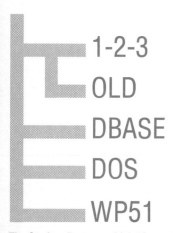

1-2-3
OLD
DBASE
DOS
WP51

The Student Resource Disk Directories
The *Student Resource Disk* directories are organized as shown here.

resume scrolling. Practice these commands until you can pause the screen before all the files scroll past.

FINISHING UP

15. Either continue to the next activity or quit for the day.

➤ Q U I C K   R E F E R E N C E

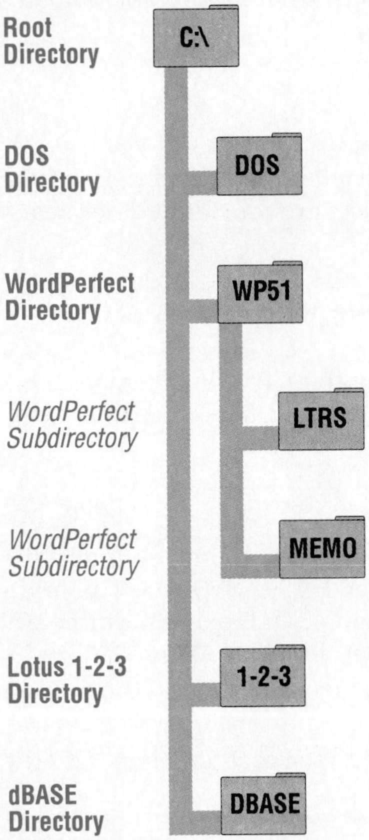

Root Directory — C:\

DOS Directory — DOS

WordPerfect Directory — WP51

WordPerfect Subdirectory — LTRS

WordPerfect Subdirectory — MEMO

Lotus 1-2-3 Directory — 1-2-3

dBASE Directory — DBASE

Directory Trees
Directories and subdirectories are organized into a treelike hierarchy. The topmost directory is called the root directory. Directories below the root directory are called directories. When directories are subdivided into additional directories, they are called subdirectories.

Any disk may be divided into directories and subdirectories. You will often find floppy disks with directories, and almost every hard disk has them. To work with these disks, you have to know how to move between directories and see how they are organized.

Changing Directories
To change directories on the current drive, you use the CHDIR or CD command. To change the default directory, type **CD**<*drive:\directory*> and press [Enter←]. If you are changing more than one level, list the directories in order, separated by a backslash. There are several versions of these commands. For example, in the figure "Moving Through Directories," the following commands would work:

- To make the subdirectory OLD the default directory, you would type **CD\\LETTERS\\OLD** and press [Enter←].
- To move up one directory, for example, from OLD to LETTERS, you would type **CD..** and press [Enter←].
- To move down to a subdirectory within the current directory, for example, from LETTERS to NEW, you would type **CD NEW**.
- To return to the root directory from any other directory, you would type **CD** and press [Enter←].

To display the default directory on the current drive, type **CD** and press [Enter←]. To display the current default directory on another drive, type **CD** followed by the drive identifier, and press [Enter←]. For example, to display the current directory on drive C, type **CD C:** and press [Enter←].

→ K E Y / S t r o k e s

Changing Directories
- To move to a directory, type **CD**<*directory*> and press [Enter←].
- To return to the root directory, type **CD** and press [Enter←].
- To move up one level, type **CD..** and press [Enter←].
- To move down one level, type **CD** <*directory*> and press [Enter←].
- To display the current directory, type **CD** and press [Enter←].
- To display the default directory on drive C, type **CD C:** and press [Enter←].

Displaying Files
To list your hard disk's organization, you use the TREE command (an external command). For a list of the directories and the files they

contain, you use the /F switch: TREE/F. This command, unlike the DIR command, lists files in all directories.

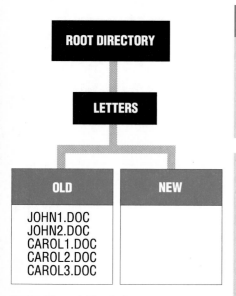

Moving Through Directories
This figure shows the root directory, a LETTERS directory, and two subdirectories, OLD and NEW.

→ KEY / S t r o k e s

Listing Directories and Files

■ To display a list of directories, type **TREE** and press [Enter←].
■ To display a list of directories and the files they contain, type **TREE/F** and press [Enter←].

TIPS

■ When you change the default directory on one drive, and then change default drives, the directory on the previous drive remains set as the default for that drive. When you switch back to that drive, you return to that directory. If you copy files to that drive without specifying otherwise, they are copied to the current default directory.
■ Most directory and file management commands work only within the current directory. For example, if you used the ERASE *.* command in a subdirectory, it would erase files only in that subdirectory, not on the entire disk.

▶ E X E R C I S E

EXERCISE 1

PRINTING A DIRECTORY TREE

1. Use the TREE command to display the tree for the original *Student Resource Disk.*
2. Use the TREE/F command to display the directories and files on the same disk.
3. Describe how the two commands differ.

Making and Removing Directories

After completing this topic, you will be able to:
- Make directories on your own disks
- Remove directories on your own disks

To organize your work on a hard disk drive, you create directories. When the directories are no longer needed, you remove them (after deleting all the files they contain). When creating directories, you should have a plan.

- Keep only essential files in the root directory.
- Store all program files related to a program in their own directory. For example, you might want a directory for DOS, 1-2-3, WordPerfect, and dBASE.
- Do not store the data files that you create in the same directory as the program files. Keep all related data files in their own directories. For example, you might have separate directories for letters, reports, financial documents, and name and address lists. You might also create separate directories for the files you create with different programs. For example, you might have separate directories for WordPerfect documents, 1-2-3 worksheets, or dBASE database files.
- Do not create too many levels since it takes time to move around them. Most disks can be well organized with no more than three levels, including the root directory.

▷ T U T O R I A L

In this tutorial, you create and remove subdirectories on the disk labeled *Resource Disk—Backup.*

GETTING STARTED

1. Load DOS so the command prompt is displayed.
2. Insert the disk labeled *Resource Disk—Backup* into drive A, and make that the default drive.
3. Type **PROMPT PG** and press Enter⏎ so that the prompt will indicate the drive and directory that you are in.

The Student Resource Disk—Backup Directories
This figure shows the organization of the directories and subdirectories that you create and remove in this tutorial.

CREATING DIRECTORIES

4. Type **MD\LETTERS** and press [Enter↵] to create a directory named LETTERS.
5. Type **MD\MEMOS** and press [Enter↵] to create a directory named MEMOS.
6. Type **MD\REPORTS** and press [Enter↵] to create a directory named REPORTS.
7. Type **DIR *.** and press [Enter↵] to see that the three new directories are listed.

CREATING SUBDIRECTORIES

8. Type **MD\LETTERS\NEW** and press [Enter↵] to create a subdirectory named NEW below the directory named LETTERS.
9. Type **MD\LETTERS\OLD** and press [Enter↵] to create a subdirectory named OLD below the directory named LETTERS.

MOVING DOWN THROUGH DIRECTORIES

10. Type **CD\LETTERS** and press [Enter↵] to move down to the LETTERS directory, and the prompt reads *A:\LETTERS>*.
11. Type **DIR** and press [Enter↵] to see that the directory contains the two new subdirectories, NEW and OLD.
12. Type **CD NEW** and press [Enter↵] to move down to the NEW subdirectory, and the prompt reads *A:\LETTERS\NEW>*.

MOVING UP THROUGH DIRECTORIES

13. Type **CD..** and press [Enter↵] to move up one level, and the prompt reads *A:\LETTERS>* to indicate that you have moved up to the LETTERS directory.
14. Type **CD** and press [Enter↵] to return to the root directory, and the prompt now reads *A:\>*.

JUMPING BETWEEN DIRECTORIES

15. Type **CD\LETTERS\NEW** and press [Enter↵] to move down to the NEW subdirectory in one step.
16. Type **CD\LETTERS\OLD** and press [Enter↵] to move directly to the OLD subdirectory.
17. Type **CD..** and press [Enter↵] to move up one level to the LETTERS directory.
18. Type **CD NEW** and press [Enter↵] to move back down to the NEW subdirectory.

REMOVING DIRECTORIES

19. Type **CD** and press [Enter↵] to move back up to the root directory in one step.
20. Type **RD\LETTERS** and press [Enter↵] to remove the LETTERS directory, and a message indicates that you cannot do so because the current directory is not empty. (It still contains subdirectories.)
21. Type **RD\LETTERS\NEW** and press [Enter↵] to remove the NEW subdirectory.

22. Type **RD\LETTERS\OLD** and press [Enter↵] to remove the OLD subdirectory.

23. Type **RD\LETTERS** and press [Enter↵] to remove the LETTERS directory.

24. Type **RD\MEMOS** and press [Enter↵] to remove the MEMOS directory.

25. Type **RD\REPORTS** and press [Enter↵] to remove the REPORTS directory.

26. Type **DIR *.** and press [Enter↵]. The message reads *File not found* because there are no directories.

FINISHING UP

27. Either continue to the next activity or quit for the day.

► Q U I C K   R E F E R E N C E

To organize your disk, you need to make and remove directories.

Making Directories

To make a directory, you use the internal command MKDIR <*directory name*> (or MD <*directory name*>). Directory names follow the same conventions that you use for filenames. However, you should not use a period and extension, or you might confuse directories with filenames at some later date. Files and subdirectories in one directory can have the same names as files and subdirectories in other directories.

The form of the command depends on whether you are working in the directory below which you want to make a directory or subdirectory. For example, if you wanted to create the directories shown in the figure "Making Directories," you would type:

Making Directories
This tree shows the root directory, a LETTERS, MEMOS, and REPORTS directory, and two subdirectories of the LETTERS directory, NEW and OLD.

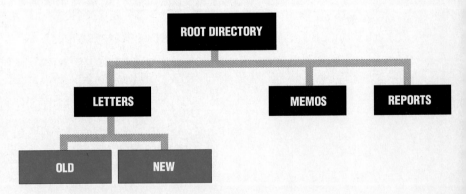

- **MD\LETTERS** and press [Enter↵]
- **MD\MEMOS** and press [Enter↵]
- **MD\REPORTS** and press [Enter↵]

To make the two subdirectories off the LETTERS directory, you would type:

- **MD\LETTERS\NEW** and press [Enter↵]
- **MD\LETTERS\OLD** and press [Enter↵]

If you had first changed directories so that LETTERS was the default directory, you could make the two subdirectories by typing:

- **MD NEW** and pressing (Enter ←)
- **MD OLD** and pressing (Enter ←)

→ | K E Y / S t r o k e s

Making Directories

- To create a directory below the root directory regardless of the directory you are in, type **MD** *<directory name>*.
- To create a directory below the root directory of another drive, type **MD** *<drive:\directory name>*. For example, to create a directory named 1-2-3 on drive C when drive B is the default drive, type **MD C:\1-2-3** and press (Enter ←).
- To create a subdirectory in the current directory, type **MD** *<directory name>*. For example, to create a subdirectory named BUDGETS below the 1-2-3 directory when 1-2-3 is the current default directory, type **MD BUDGETS** and press (Enter ←).

Removing Directories

To remove a directory, you use the internal command RMDIR *<directory name>* (or RD *<directory name>*). For example, to delete a directory named LETTERS, you would type **RD LETTERS** and press (Enter ←). To delete a subdirectory named NEW below a directory named LETTERS, you would type **RD LETTERS\NEW** and press (Enter ←). The directory you want to remove must not contain any files or subdirectories, and it cannot be the current default directory.

▶ | E X E R C I S E

EXERCISE 1

CREATING AND DELETING DIRECTORIES

1. Insert the disk labeled *Resource Disk—Backup* into one of the disk drives, and make it the default drive.
2. Create a directory named 1992.
3. Create two subdirectories in the 1992 directory named SALES and BUDGETS.
4. Display a tree of the directories.
5. Delete all the new directories and subdirectories from the disk.
6. Display another tree of the directories.

Specifying Paths

After completing this topic, you will be able to:
- Explain what a path is
- Specify paths in your own commands
- Use the XCOPY command with paths to copy files in subdirectories

In previous topics, you frequently specified source and target drives when executing commands that copied, moved, or deleted files. When a disk is divided into directories, you not only must specify a drive, you also must specify a directory or directories in many commands. Specifying the drive and directories is called specifying a path.

Paths are simply a listing of the directories and subdirectories that specify exactly where a file can be found or where it is to be copied to. It is like telling someone that "the letter to ACME Hardware is in the manila folder labeled ACME in the hanging folder labeled Hardware in the third file cabinet from the right." These precise instructions make it easy to locate the file.

▶ T U T O R I A L

In this tutorial, you use paths to copy files on the *Resource Disk—Backup.*

GETTING STARTED

1. Load DOS so that the command prompt is displayed.
2. Insert the disk labeled *Resource Disk—Backup* into drive A, and make that the default drive.

CREATING DIRECTORIES

3. Type **MD\WP51** and press [Enter←].
4. Type **MD\TEXT** and press [Enter←].
5. Type **MD\TEXT\BATCH** and press [Enter←].
6. Type **DIR *.** and press [Enter←] to display the new directories but not the BATCH subdirectory.

COPYING FILES

7. Type **COPY A:CHPT?.WP5   A:\WP51** and press [Enter←] to copy the files into the WP51 directory.

8. Type **DIR A:\WP51** and press Enter↵ to see that the files were copied into the WP51 directory.
9. Type **COPY A:*.TXT A:\TEXT** and press Enter↵ to copy the files into the TEXT directory.
10. Type **DIR A:\TEXT** and press Enter↵ to see that the files were copied into the TEXT directory.
11. Type **COPY A:*.BAT A:\TEXT\BATCH** and press Enter↵ to copy the files into the BATCH subdirectory below the TEXT directory.
12. Type **DIR A:\TEXT\BATCH** and press Enter↵ to see that the files were copied into the BATCH subdirectory.

ERASING FILES IN THE WP51 DIRECTORY

13. Type **DIR A:\WP51*.*** and press Enter↵ to preview which files would be deleted with the path and filename specification.
14. Type **ERASE A:\WP51*.*** and press Enter↵. In a few moments, the prompt reads *Are you sure (Y/N)?*.
15. Press Y and then Enter↵ to delete the files.
16. Type **DIR A:\WP51** and press Enter↵ to see that the directory is now empty. The two listings, . *<DIR>* and .. *<DIR>*, indicate hidden files.

ERASING FILES IN THE TEXT DIRECTORY

17. Type **DIR A:\TEXT*.*** and press Enter↵ to preview which files would be deleted with the path and filename specification.
18. Type **ERASE A:\TEXT*.*** and press Enter↵. In a few moments, the prompt reads *Are you sure (Y/N)?*.
19. Press Y and then Enter↵ to delete the files.
20. Type **DIR A:\TEXT** and press Enter↵ to see that the directory is now empty except for the BATCH subdirectory.

ERASING FILES IN THE BATCH SUBDIRECTORY

21. Type **DIR A:\TEXT\BATCH*.*** and press Enter↵ to preview which files would be deleted with the path and filename specification.
22. Type **ERASE A:\TEXT\BATCH*.*** and press Enter↵. In a few moments, the prompt reads *Are you sure (Y/N)?*.
23. Press Y and then Enter↵ to delete the files.
24. Type **DIR A:\TEXT\BATCH** and press Enter↵ to see that the directory is now empty. The two listings, . *<DIR>* and .. *<DIR>*, indicate hidden files.

FINISHING UP

25. Either continue to the next activity or quit for the day.

> **QUICK REFERENCE**

To specify a path, you must indicate the drive, then the name of all subdirectories leading to the file, and then the filename. All elements

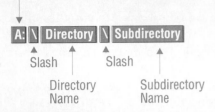

Drive Identifier

Slash   Slash

Directory   Subdirectory
Name   Name

Specifying Paths
When specifying a path, you use a drive identifier and then list a directory and any subdirectories. Each item is separated from the next by a backslash.

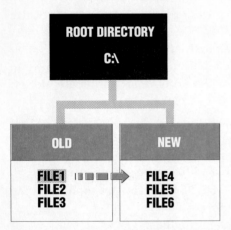

COPY C:\OLD\FILE1 C:\NEW

Paths
When copying files, displaying directories, or deleting files from the command prompt, you have to specify a path when the source or target directory is not the default.

must be separated from one another by backslashes (\), for example, C:\LETTER\NEW\FILE1.DOC.

When specifying paths, you have to consider both the source and target directories:

■ If the source directory is the default, you have to specify only the source filename and the path to the target.
■ If the target directory is the default, you have to specify only the path to the source and the source filename.
■ If neither the target nor the source directory is the default, you have to specify the path for both.

For example, let's assume your disk has the directories and files shown in the figure "Paths."

■ To copy files, you have to specify a path only when the source or target directory is not the default.
  • When OLD is the default, the path you specify to copy FILE1 to the NEW directory is only for the target. For example, type **COPY FILE1 C:\NEW**.
  • When NEW is the default, the path you specify to copy FILE1 to the NEW directory is only for the source. For example, type **COPY C:\OLD\FILE1**.
  • When the root directory is the default, the paths you specify to copy FILE1 to the NEW directory are for both the source and the target. For example, type **COPY C:\OLD\FILE1 C:\NEW**.

■ To display a list of the filenames in a directory, the same principles work.
  • When the root directory is the default, you can display its directory by just typing **DIR** and pressing [Enter←].
  • To display the files in the OLD directory, you type **DIR C:\OLD** and press [Enter←].
  • To display the files in the NEW directory, you type **DIR C:\NEW** and press [Enter←].

■ To delete a file, the same principles also work. For example, when OLD is the default directory:
  • To delete FILE1, you type **DEL FILE1** and press [Enter←].
  • To delete FILE4 in the NEW subdirectory, you type **DEL C:\NEW\FILE4** and press [Enter←].

The XCOPY Command
Your can use the XCOPY command to copy files in subdirectories, files created after a certain date, or only files that weren't copied previously using the switches described in the table "XCOPY Switches." For example:

■ To copy all files on a disk in drive C to a disk in drive A, type **XCOPY C:\ A:\/S**.
■ To copy all files in the 1-2-3 directory on drive C, and all its subdirectories, to a disk in drive A, type **XCOPY C:\1-2-3 A:/S**.
■ To copy just the files in the root directory on the disk in drive C to a disk in drive A, type **XCOPY C:\ A:**.
■ To copy just the files in the 1-2-3 directory on drive C, without copying files in any of its subdirectories, type **XCOPY C:\1-2-3 A:**.

ARCHIVE BITS

When you create a file, DOS sets one of its bits—the archive bit—to 1 to indicate that it is a new file. If you then copy the file with the XCOPY command using the /M switch, DOS changes the archive bit to 0, to indicate that the file has been copied. If you later revise the file and save it again, DOS changes the archive bit back to 1, to show that it is a new file. This property of the /M switch means that you can use it repeatedly and have DOS XCOPY only those files that have not been changed since the last time you used it, ignoring all files that it has previously copied.

If you want to change the archive bit back from 0 to 1 manually, you can do it with the ATTRIB *<filename or wildcard>* +A command. For example, to reset the archive bit to 1 for every file in the current directory with the extension .DOC, type **ATTRIB *.DOC +A** and press Enter⏎.

- To copy all files on a disk in drive C, with a date later than December 31, 1992, to a disk in drive A, type **XCOPY C:\ A:\/S/ D:12-31-92**.
- To copy all files on a disk in drive C that have been changed since you last used the XCOPY command to a disk in drive A, type **XCOPY C:\ A:\/S/M**.

XCOPY SWITCHES

Switch	Description
/P	Prompts you before copying each file.
/D:mm-dd-yy	Copies only files created on or after the specified date.
/W	Waits for you to insert a disk and press any key before copying.
/S	Copies all files in the source directory and its subdirectories.
/E	Creates subdirectories on the target to match those on the source.
/V	Verifies that files are copied correctly.
/M	Copies only those files whose archive bit is 1; after the file has been copied, the archive bit for the source file is set to 0. (The archive bit is a marker that indicates if a file has been backed up or not.) When using this switch, the source disk cannot be write-protected.
/A	Same as /M but does not change the archive bit for the source file.

XCOPY with the /M switch is very useful for copying files when the target disk does not have enough room for all the files on the source. Say you want to copy all the files in the 123 directory of drive C to a disk in drive A but a disk in that drive won't hold all of them. Type **XCOPY C: \123 A: /M**. When the first disk is full, the message *Insufficient disk space* is displayed and the command prompt reappears. Put a new floppy into the drive and repeat the XCOPY command (press F3). XCOPY will copy another diskful of files, but it will not copy any files it has already copied, because the /M switch changed their archive bit to 0 after copying them. Continue to do this until all the files have been copied and the command prompt reappears without the *Insufficient disk space* message. If you want XCOPY to copy the files in subdirectories of the source directory too with this procedure, remember to use the /S switch along with the /M one. If you want it to create subdirectories to match those of the source disk even if those subdirectories are empty, use the /E switch too.

►EXERCISE

EXERCISE 1

PRINTING DIRECTORIES

1. Insert the *Student Resource Disk* into drive A.
2. Change the default drive to A.
3. Without changing the default directory, use the DIR command to display a directory of all the files in the root directory and the subdirectories on the disk.

REVIEW

- A disk can be divided into directories and subdirectories. The highest-level directory is called the root directory.
- To change directories, you use the CD or CHDIR command. For example, to change to a directory named LETTERS, you type **CD\LETTERS** and press Enter⏎.
- To display a list of directories on a hard disk drive, you use the TREE command. To display a list of directories and the files they contain, you use the TREE/F command.
- The command you use to make new directories on a disk is MKDIR (or MD), which is an internal command.
- The command you use to remove a directory is RD or RMDIR, which is an internal command. You can remove a directory only if it is empty—that is, it can't contain files or subdirectories.
- To specify a path, you specify the drive and any directories between the root directory and the file. For example, to copy a file named FILENAME on drive C from the directory LETTERS to the directory MEMOS, type **COPY C:\LETTERS\FILENAME C:\MEMOS**.

CHAPTER 4 QUESTIONS

FILL IN THE BLANK

1. To move to a directory named LETTERS on drive C, you would enter the command _____.
2. To move to a directory named OLD below a directory named LETTERS on drive C, you would enter the command _____.
3. To move back to the root directory from any subdirectory, you would enter the command _____.
4. To move up one level in the directory tree, you would enter the command _____.
5. To create a directory named LETTERS on drive C, you would enter the command _____.
6. To create a directory named OLD below a directory named LETTERS on drive C, you would enter the command _____.
7. To remove a directory named LETTERS on drive C, you would enter the command _____.
8. To remove a directory named OLD below a directory named LETTERS on drive C, you would enter the command _____.
9. To copy a file named JOHN.DOC to a directory named LETTERS on drive C, you would enter the command _____.

10. To copy a file named JOHN.DOC to a directory named OLD below a directory named LETTERS on drive C, you would enter the command _____.

MATCH THE COLUMNS

1. CD\
2. CD ..
3. <DIR>
4. [1-2-3]
5. TREE
6. TREE/F
7. MD
8. RD
9. C:\TEXT\BATCH

__ Indicates a directory when you use the DIR/W command

__ Displays a list of directories, subdirectories, and files

__ Returns you to the root directory

__ A path to a subdirectory on drive C

__ Makes a directory

__ Indicates a directory when you use the DIR command

__ Moves you up one level in the directories

__ Displays a list of directories and subdirectories

__ Removes a directory

WRITE OUT THE ANSWERS

1. What is the topmost directory on a disk called?
2. What command do you use to change directories? What command do you use to move up one level? Are these internal or external commands?
3. What must you do before you can remove a directory from a hard disk?
4. What command do you use when you want to display the directories on a hard disk? When you want to display both the directories and the files?
5. What command do you use to make directories?
6. What command do you use to remove directories?
7. If you wanted to create a directory named FIRST below the root directory, what command would you use?
8. If you wanted to create a subdirectory named SECOND below the directory named FIRST, what command would you use?
9. If the SECOND directory was the current default directory, what two commands could you use to create a new subdirectory below it named THIRD?
10. To copy a file named JONES from the root directory of drive A to a directory named LETTERS on drive C, what command would you use?
11. To display a listing of the files in a subdirectory named SECOND below a directory named FIRST, what command would you use from the root directory?

PROJECTS

PROJECT 1

PLANNING AND DRAWING A DIRECTORY TREE

Sketch out a directory tree for the following directories and subdirectories. Name each of the directories and subdirectories as you see fit.

1. The root directory is drive C.
2. Below the root directory are directories for DOS, Lotus 1-2-3, WordPerfect 5.1, dBASE III Plus, budgets, reports, memos, and letters.
3. Below the budgets, reports, memos, and letters directories are subdirectories for 1993, 1994, and 1995.

PROJECT 2

CREATING A DOS REFERENCE CARD

The table "Summary of DOS Commands" lists some of the most frequently used DOS command procedures. Complete the table by entering in the Command column the command you would use to perform each of the tasks. In the Type column, indicate if the command is an internal or external command.

SUMMARY OF DOS COMMANDS

Description	Command	Type
Making and Changing Directories		
Creates a new directory	_____	_____
Changes the default directory	_____	_____
Removes a directory	_____	_____
Returns to the root directory	_____	_____
Returns to one level up	_____	_____
Displays a list of directories	_____	_____
Displays a list of directories and files	_____	_____

Advanced DOS Procedures

Checking Disks and Files

> **After completing this topic, you will be able to:**
> - Explain why disks should be checked periodically
> - Check disks and files on your own system

```
B:\PART1.DOC
Contains 3 non-contiguous blocks
B:\PART2.DOC
Contains 2 non-contiguous blocks
```

The CHKDSK Command
If you use the CHKDSK *.* command and get a message that your disk contains noncontiguous blocks, you need to unfragment your disk.

When you save a file on a new disk, it is stored neatly on adjacent sectors around adjacent tracks on the disk. But after the disk begins to fill up and you delete some files and add others, the disk drive has to work harder to store a file. It tends to store different parts of the file wherever it can find free sectors. After a while, a file may end up scattered all over the disk on noncontiguous blocks (parts of the file that do not adjoin each other on the disk). Files stored this way are called fragmented files.

When files are stored in widely separated sectors, some blocks may get lost and not be retrievable. Moreover, the drive's read/write head will have to move back and forth more frequently. This puts increased wear and tear on the drive because the drive's read/write head must keep moving over the disk's surface to reach parts of the files. It also slows down any save and retrieve operations.

To determine if files are fragmented, use the CHKDSK command. To correct the disk, copy all files onto another disk using the COPY *.* command. If the disk contains subdirectories, use the XCOPY command with the /S switch.

▶ TUTORIAL

In this tutorial, you check the disk labeled *Resource Disk—Backup.*

GETTING STARTED

1. Load DOS so that the command prompt is displayed.
2. Insert your disks as follows:
   - On a hard disk system, insert the disk labeled *Resource Disk— Backup* into drive A.
   - On a floppy disk system, insert the disk that contains the CHKDSK.COM or CHKDSK.EXE file into drive A and the disk labeled *Resource Disk—Backup* into drive B.

3. Set your drives as follows:
   - On a hard disk system, make drive C the default drive.
   - On a floppy disk system, make drive A the default drive.

CHECKING A DISK

4. Enter a command as follows:
   - On a hard disk system, type **CHKDSK A:** and press (Enter←).
   - On a floppy disk system, type **CHKDSK B:** and press (Enter←).

   When you use this command, the screen indicates the following information about your system:
   - The total disk space, the space allocated to data files, and the remaining space available on the disk
   - The size and number of hidden files (if any)
   - The size and number of directories
   - The size and number of user files
   - If you are using DOS 4 or 5, the number of bytes in each allocation unit, the total number of allocation units, and the remaining allocation units available for new files
   - The total memory in the computer and the amount that is currently free (not occupied by programs or data)

CHECKING THE FILES ON A DISK

5. Enter a command as follows:
   - On a hard disk system, type **CHKDSK A:*.*** and press (Enter←).
   - On a floppy disk system, type **CHKDSK B:*.*** and press (Enter←).

   If all the files on the disk are contiguous, a message reads *All specified file(s) are contiguous.* If some are not, a series of messages tells you which files contain noncontiguous blocks.

FINISHING UP

6. Either continue to the next activity or quit for the day.

▶ QUICK   REFERENCE

To check a disk, you use the CHKDSK command (an external command). You can also use variations of the CHKDSK command to check individual files. For example:

- To check a single file, type **CHKDSK B:**<*filename*> (where <*filename*>is the name of the file).
- To list the names of files as they are being checked, use the /V switch. For example, to list the names of all files on drive B as they are being checked, type **CHKDSK B:/V**.
- To check the status of all files on a disk, type **CHKDSK B:*.*** and press (Enter←). This command gives you the same information as the other CHKDSK commands but also tells you if all files occupy contiguous, or adjacent, blocks (as they should) or lists the files

Contiguous and Noncontiguous Sectors

Disks with files located in contiguous sectors put less wear and tear on the drive and allow faster file saving and retrieving.

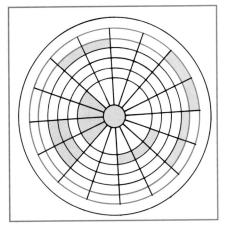

When a file is stored in noncontiguous sectors, parts of it are scattered about the disk. For the disk drive to retrieve such a file, it must move back and forth all over the disk.

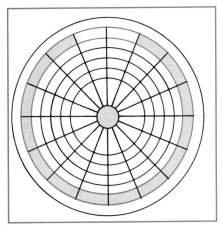

When a file is stored in contiguous sectors, it is stored on the disk in adjacent sectors. The disk drive can retrieve such a file in one smooth, continuous operation.

that contain noncontiguous, or scattered, blocks as shown in the figure "The CHKDSK Command."

If your disk contains noncontiguous blocks, you should copy the files to a new disk so that they are contiguous. To do so, copy all the files to a new formatted disk with the COPY *.* or XCOPY /S command. You can also use utility programs such as Norton Ulitities to move files together into contiguous sectors. This is the only practical way to do it on hard disks.

→ **KEY/Strokes**

Checking the Files on a Disk

1. On a floppy disk system, insert the DOS disk that contains the CHKDSK.COM or CHKDSK.EXE file into drive A, and make that the default drive.
2. Insert your disks as follows:
   - On a hard disk system, insert the disk you want to check into drive A.
   - On a floppy disk system, insert the disk you want to check into drive B.
3. Enter one of the following commands:
   - On a hard disk system, type:
     - **CHKDSK A:** and press [Enter ↵] to check the disk
     - **CHKDSK A*.*** and press [Enter ↵] to check files on the disk
     - **CHKDSK A:/V** and press [Enter ↵] to list files as they are checked
   - On a floppy disk system, type:
     - **CHKDSK B:** and press [Enter ↵] to check the disk
     - **CHKDSK B*.*** and press [Enter ↵] to check files on the disk
     - **CHKDSK B:/V** and press [Enter ↵] to list files as they are checked

TIPS

- If sectors of a file become scattered, the operating system may not be able to find sections called allocation units, or blocks. The CHKDSK command occasionally displays the following message:

  ```
  Errors found, F parameter not specified
  Corrections will not be written to disk

  Convert lost chains to files (Y/N)?
  4096 bytes disk space would be freed
  ```

- If you see this message, press [N] and then [Enter ↵] to return to the command prompt. Type **CHKDSK /F** and press [Enter ↵]. When the message reappears, press [Y] and then [Enter ↵] to store the lost allocation units in one or more files named

FILEnnnn.CHK (where nnnn is a sequential number) in the root directory. You can then retrieve these files to see if any contain useful data that you want to recover. You can retrieve these files with any application program that reads ASCII text files, or you can see their contents with the command TYPE FILE<*nnnn*>.CHK or TYPE FILE<*nnnn*>.CHK | MORE.

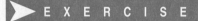

EXERCISE

EXERCISE 1

CHECKING DISKS

Check any of your disks with the CHKDSK, CHKDSK *.*, and CHKDSK/V commands.

Displaying and Printing ASCII Text Files

After completing this topic, you will be able to:
- Describe the different types of files that your system creates
- Display and print ASCII text files from DOS
- Stop a print job or remove files from the print queue

Files on the disk that are in ASCII text format can be displayed on the screen or printed from DOS. To understand ASCII text files, you have to understand something about the other files that you create with your application programs.

Binary files contain formatting codes specific to the application program that created them. For example, when you underline words, add page numbers, change margins or line spacing, or add headers and footers, you are actually entering codes into the document. These format codes are specific to the program you are using; there is no established standard. Thus these codes cannot be interpreted by other programs, which have their own codes. To use binary files with another program, the program-specific codes must be either removed or converted into codes the other program will understand. This is generally done by saving them with a command designed for this purpose or by using a separate program to convert them.

ASCII files are saved in a standard format understood by almost all programs. They can thus be used by other programs or easily transmitted by a modem over telephone lines. Since binary files can rarely be interpreted by other programs or telecommunicated by modem without first making special provisions, many programs let you save files for these purposes as ASCII text files. When files are saved in this way, all format codes specific to the program are removed. These files are identified with a variety of extensions, the most common being .TXT (for text).

Print files are like ASCII files, but all format codes are interpreted rather than removed. A print file is created just like a printout on the printer. The only difference is that the output is sent to a file on a disk instead of to the printer. For example, headers, footers, page numbers, top and bottom margins, and other formats that would appear on a printout also appear in the print file on the disk. Print files can also be printed directly from the operating system and, in some cases, can be used by other programs. For example, you can print a Lotus 1-2-3 file to the disk and then retrieve it into a WordPerfect document. Print files are usually identified with an extension such as .PRT or .PRN.

In this tutorial, you display ASCII text files on the *Student Resource Disk* and create an ASCII text file using the COPY CON command. You also print an ASCII text file named README.TXT from the command prompt. README files are frequently put on program disks to inform users of changes that have been made since the program's user manual was printed. Before you can use the PRINT command to send output to your printer, you need to know what port it is connected to. Typical ports are LPT1, LPT2, COM1, or COM2. Ask which yours is connected to and write it down so that you won't forget it. If it is not LPT1, substitute its name for PRN in the steps that follow.

GETTING STARTED

1. Load DOS so that the command prompt is displayed.
2. Insert the original *Student Resource Disk* into drive A.
3. Make drive A the default drive.

DISPLAYING ASCII TEXT FILES

4. Type **TYPE WHATSUP.DOC** and press Enter↵ to display the file on the screen.
5. Now repeat the same command. (You can press F3 and then Enter↵ to do so.) Practice pressing Ctrl-S or Pause to pause the display. After pausing, press any key to continue. Repeat the procedure a few times until you are comfortable with it.
6. Type **TYPE ASCII.TXT** and press Enter↵ to scroll an illustration of the characters in the IBM PC character onto the screen.

PRINTING THE README.TXT FILE

7. On a floppy disk system, insert the DOS disk with the PRINT.COM or PRINT.EXE file into drive A. Insert the *Student Resource Disk* into drive B.
8. Enter a command as follows:
   ■ On a hard disk system, type **PRINT A:README.TXT** and press Enter↵.
   ■ On a floppy disk system, type **PRINT B:README.TXT** and press Enter↵.

   The first time you use the PRINT command in a session, the prompt may read *Name of list device [PRN]:*. If this happens, press Enter↵ to answer the prompt for the name of the list device or type the name of the port your printer is connected to, and then press Enter↵. The message then reads *Resident part of PRINT installed, x:\README.TXT is currently being printed*. In a moment, the text file is printed on your printer, and then the command prompt reappears.

CREATING AN ASCII TEXT FILE

9. Type **COPY CON MYFILE.TXT** and press Enter↵.
10. Type **This is my first text file created from DOS** and press Enter↵.

11. Type **I press Enter to end lines of text** and press [Enter←].
12. Type **and press F6 when finished**.
13. Press [F6] to end the batch file, and a ^Z is displayed.
14. Press [Enter←] to save the file, and the message *1 File(s) copied* is displayed.
15. Type **TYPE MYFILE.TXT** and press [Enter←] to display the ASCII text file that you created.

16. Either continue to the next activity or quit for the day.

> **QUICK REFERENCE**

To display and print ASCII files, you use the TYPE and PRINT commands.

Displaying ASCII Text Files
To display an ASCII text file from the command prompt, you use the internal TYPE command. To do so, type **TYPE** <*filename*> and press [Enter←]. Sometimes long files scroll by too fast to read. You can pause the screen while it is scrolling by pressing [Ctrl]-[S] or [Pause]. To resume scrolling, press any key.

Printing ASCII Text Files
To print an ASCII text file from the command prompt, you use the external PRINT command. To do so, type **PRINT** <*filename*> and press [Enter←]. The first time you use this command in a session, a prompt asks you for the name of the print device and suggests PRN. If your printer is attached to the LPT1 port, you just press [Enter←] to print the file. If your printer is attached to a different port, for example, LPT2, COM1, or COM2, you type the name of the port, and press [Enter←].

This command allows you to send one job after another to the printer. If one isn't finished printing before the next arrives, the new file is added to a print queue, which is just a list of jobs waiting to be processed. PRINT is also a background program. When you use this command to print files, you can continue working on other tasks while your files are being printed.

When printing files from the command prompt, you can use additional commands:

- To display a list of files in the print queue if there is more than one, type **PRINT** and press [Enter←].
- To stop printing a file, type **PRINT/T** (for "terminate") and press [Enter←]. This command removes all jobs from the print queue.
- To remove a single file from the print queue, type **PRINT** <*filename*> **/C** (for "cancel") (where <*filename*> is the name of the file to be removed from the queue). For example, to cancel a job named FILENAME.EXT, type **PRINT FILENAME.EXT/C**.

→ K E Y / S t r o k e s

Printing ASCII Text Files

1. Insert your disks as follows:
   - On a hard disk system, insert the disk with the ASCII text file into drive A.
   - On a floppy disk system, insert the DOS disk with the PRINT.COM or PRINT.EXE file into drive A and the disk with the ASCII text file into drive B.
2. Set your drives as follows:
   - On a hard disk system, make drive C the default drive.
   - On a floppy disk system, make drive A the default drive.
3. Enter the command as follows:
   - On a hard disk system, type **PRINT A:**<*filename.ext*> and press [Enter←].
   - On a floppy disk system, type **PRINT B:**<*filename.ext*> and press [Enter←].

   The prompt may read *Name of list device [PRN]:*. If this happens, press [Enter←] to answer the prompt for the name of the list device or type the name of the port your printer is connected to, and then press [Enter←]. The message then reads *Resident part of PRINT installed, B:filename.ext is currently being printed.*

➤ E X E R C I S E S

EXERCISE 1

DISPLAYING TEXT FILES

Use the TYPE command to display the following ASCII text files: ASCII.TXT, WHATSUP.DOC, and JUMPSTRT.BAT.

EXERCISE 2

DISPLAYING BINARY FILES

The file BANKLOAN.WK1 is a binary file saved with the Lotus 1-2-3 program. Use the TYPE command to display it from the command prompt. Describe what happens.

EXERCISE 3

PRINTING A 1-2-3 PRINT FILE

The BANKLOAN.PRN file on the original *Student Resource Disk* is a Lotus 1-2-3 print file. Use the PRINT command to make a printout of this file from the command prompt.

EXERCISE 4

PRINTING THE WHATSUP.DOC FILE

Use the PRINT command to make a printout of the WHATSUP.DOC file from the command prompt.

Using Redirection and Filters

After completing this topic, you will be able to:
- Send lists of files displayed with the DIR command to the printer and to a file on the disk
- Sort filenames on the disk
- Pause lists so that they don't scroll off the screen

DOS has several commands that allow you to manage your files better. The basic procedures involve using filters, pipes, and redirection commands. Filters sort files or directory listings or pause text that scrolls across the screen too quickly for you to read. Pipes send the output of one command to another command where it is used as input. Redirection commands redirect output from its normal device to another device. For example, you can send a directory listing to the printer or to a disk file, or you can copy a file to the printer instead of to another file on the disk.

▶ T U T O R I A L

In this tutorial, you send a directory of the filenames on a disk to the printer and then to a file on the disk. (If necessary substitute the name of your output device or port for PRN in the steps that follow.)

GETTING STARTED

1. Load DOS so that the command prompt is displayed.
2. Insert your disks as follows:
   - On a hard disk system, insert the *Resource Disk—Backup* into drive A.
   - On a floppy disk system, insert the *Resource Disk—Backup* into drive B.
3. Set your drives as follows:
   - On a hard disk system, make drive A the default drive.
   - On a floppy disk system, make drive B the default drive.
4. Be sure that the printer is on and has paper in it and that the paper is aligned.

5. Type **DIR >PRN** and press ⌷Enter↲⌷ to send a directory listing to the printer. (You may have to press On Line, Form Feed (FF), and then On Line again to eject the paper from the printer.)
6. Type **DIR *.DOC>PRN** and press ⌷Enter↲⌷ to send a listing of files with the extension .DOC to the printer.

STORING DIRECTORY LISTINGS IN A DISK FILE

7. Type **DIR *.TXT >FILELIST.TXT** and press ⌷Enter↲⌷ to send a listing of files with the extension .TXT to a file named FILELIST.TXT on the disk.
8. Type **TYPE FILELIST.TXT** and press ⌷Enter↲⌷ to display the contents of the FILELIST.TXT file.
9. Type **DIR *.DOC >>FILELIST.TXT** and press ⌷Enter↲⌷ to append a list of additional files with the .DOC extension to the FILELIST.TXT file.
10. Type **TYPE FILELIST.TXT** and press ⌷Enter↲⌷ to see that the new files have been appended to the end of the file.

REDIRECTING AN ASCII TEXT FILE TO THE PRINTER

11. Type **TYPE FILELIST.TXT >PRN** and press ⌷Enter↲⌷ to print the file.

USING THE MORE FILTER

12. On a floppy disk system, insert the disk with the MORE.COM file into drive A and the *Resource Disk—Backup* into drive B.
13. Reset your drives as follows:
    - On a hard disk system, make drive C the default drive.
    - On a floppy disk system, make drive B the default drive
14. Enter a command as follows: (The | character is the split vertical bar (⌷¦⌷) on the backslash (⌷\⌷) key. You must press ⌷⇧ Shift⌷ to enter it.)
    - On a hard disk system, type **DIR A: | MORE** and press ⌷Enter↲⌷.
    - On a floppy disk system, type **DIR | A:MORE** and press ⌷Enter↲⌷.
    The directory is listed on the screen until the screen is full. The screen stops scrolling at that point, and the message -- *More* -- is displayed on the last line.
15. Press any key to continue scrolling the list.
16. Enter a command as follows:
    - On a hard disk system, type **MORE <A:WHATSUP.DOC** and press ⌷Enter↲⌷.
    - On a floppy disk system, type **A:MORE <WHATSUP.DOC** and press ⌷Enter↲⌷.
    The file is displayed on the screen until the screen is full. The screen stops scrolling at that point, and the message -- *More* -- is displayed on the last line.
17. Press any key to display another screenful of the file. When the command prompt reappears, the file has been displayed in its entirety.

SORTING AND PAUSING

18. Enter a command as follows to sort the directory of drive A in alphabetical order by filename and list the names so that they do not scroll off the screen:
    - On a hard disk system, type **DIR A: |SORT |MORE** and press Enter⏎.
    - On a floppy disk system, type **DIR |A:SORT |A:MORE** and press Enter⏎.
19. Press any key to see the rest of the filenames.
20. Enter a command as follows to sort the list of files by month but not by year:
    - On a hard disk system, type **DIR A: |SORT/+24 |MORE** and press Enter⏎.
    - On a floppy disk system, type **DIR |A:SORT/+24 |A:MORE** and press Enter⏎.
21. Press any key to see the rest of the filenames.

SORTING AND PRINTING A DIRECTORY

22. Enter a command as follows to print a directory sorted by file size:
    - On a hard disk system, type **DIR A: |SORT/+14 >PRN** and press Enter⏎.
    - On a floppy disk system, type **DIR |A:SORT/+14 >PRN** and press Enter⏎.

FINISHING UP

23. Either continue to the next activity or quit for the day.

▶ QUICK REFERENCE

When working with ASCII text files, it is helpful to use commands that direct output of a command to the printer or a disk file, sort lists, and pause long file listings on the screen.

Redirecting Data

DOS commands accept input from devices like the keyboard, disks, programs, and mice. They then process the input and send it to output devices like the display or printer. The input devices and output devices that the commands use by default are called the standard devices. You can, however, specify other input and output devices. Doing so is called redirection since you direct the input or output from or to another device. For example, you can send text that is normally displayed on the screen to a printer or to a file on the disk. To redirect input and output, you use two characters, < and >.

- The > character redirects the output from a command. For example, DIR >FILELIST.TXT redirects the directory of a disk to a disk file named FILELIST.TXT and replaces that file's previous contents, if any. A special version of this command, >>, appends the output to the end of an existing file. For example, DIR >>FILELIST.TXT appends a directory of a disk to an existing file named FILELIST.TXT. If the file does not already exist, it is created. You can also use the > character with the COPY and TYPE commands to send ASCII text files to the printer. For example, to print a file named FILELIST.TXT, you could use either COPY FILELIST.TXT >PRN or TYPE FILELIST.TXT >PRN.

■ The < character directs the input to a command. For example, MORE <DIR B: redirects the output from the DIR command to the MORE filter before it is sent to the screen.

One of the most frequent uses of redirection is to send directories of the files on your disk to a printer or disk file for future reference. Here are some typical examples:

■ DIR >LPT1 or >PRN sends the directory to the printer attached to LPT1 (a port on the computer).

■ DIR >FILELIST.TXT redirects the directory of a disk to a disk file named FILELIST.TXT.

■ DIR >>FILELIST.TXT appends a directory of a disk to an existing file named FILELIST.TXT. If the file does not already exist, it is created.

■ DIR B:*.DOC >>B:FILELIST appends a directory of all files with the extension .DOC on a disk in drive B to an existing file named FILELIST.TXT on drive B. If the file does not already exist, it is created.

■ TREE >PRN sends the tree listing directories to the printer.

■ TREE/F >PRN sends the tree listing directories and files to the printer.

Filters and Pipes

Filters are programs that take the output from one command, process it in some way, and then send it to the standard output device. DOS filters include the utility programs MORE and SORT, which respectively, pause output on the screen and sort files and directories. You can use redirection along with these filters.

When you use a filter, you have to send the output from one command as input to another command. To do so, you can use redirection, but using a pipe is easier. A pipe connects two programs so that the output from the first is sent to a temporary file on the disk. The information stored in this file is then used as input for the second program. To connect the two programs, you use a pipe character ([|]). (This character is the split vertical bar found on the [\] key. To enter it, you hold down [⇧ Shift] and press that key.) For example, to sort a directory listing, you use the command **DIR | SORT** or **DIR I SORT**. (Spaces are optional.) The DIR command sends the directory listing to a temporary file on the disk, which the SORT program then sorts. The sorted directory is then sent to the standard output device, in this case, the screen. You can also redirect the output from the SORT program to the printer with the command DIR | SORT >PRN.

Pausing a Scrolling Screen Display

When you are displaying information on the screen, it frequently scrolls by so quickly that you cannot read it. When this happens, you can use the MORE command (an external command). This command specifies that output from a command be displayed a screenful at a time. When the screen is full, the message -- *More* -- is displayed. You then press any key to continue. You can also press Ctrl-Break to cancel the command. Here are some typical examples of how you use the MORE command:

- DIR | MORE displays the directory of the disk until the screen is full and then displays the message -- *More* --. You press any key to continue.
- MORE < FILENAME.EXT or TYPE FILENAME.EXT | MORE displays the specified file a screen at a time.
- TREE | MORE or TREE/F | MORE displays a directory tree a screen at a time.

The MORE command writes a temporary file on the default drive, so the disk in that drive cannot be write-protected or you will get an error message.

Sorting Files

SORT (an external command) can be used to sort the contents of a file into alphabetical or numerical order. You can sort by complete lines or specify a column that should be used to determine the order of the sort. Here are some typical examples:

- SORT <FILENAME.TXT sends the output of the file named FILENAME.TXT to the SORT command where it is processed and then displayed on your screen in sorted order.
- SORT <FILENAME.TXT>PRN sends the output of the file named FILENAME.TXT to the SORT command and then sends the results to the printer.
- SORT <FILE1.TXT>FILE2.TXT sorts the file named FILE1.TXT and then sends the output to a file named FILE2.TXT.
- SORT/R <FILE1.TXT>FILE2.TXT sorts a file named FILE1.TXT in reverse order and then sends the output to a file named FILE2.TXT.
- SORT/+10 <FILENAME.TXT sorts the specified file based on the contents of the line beginning with the tenth column, which is the extension.

> E X E R C I S E

EXERCISE 1

USING THE MORE FILTER AND REDIRECTING OUTPUT

1. Use the MORE filter to pause a TREE/F display of the files and directories on the original *Student Resource Disk*.
2. Use the >PRN redirection command to send the output from the TREE/F command to the printer.

Creating Batch Files

After completing this topic, you will be able to:
- Explain the purpose of batch files
- Create and execute batch files
- Display the contents of a batch file

With batch files, you can tell the computer to do a series of tasks by entering a single command. Suppose you want to send the directories for a series of floppy disks to a disk file so that you can print it out as a permanent record. To do so, you would insert disks into drive A one at a time and then type **DIR A: >>A:DIRLIST.TXT**. You can store these keystrokes in a batch file, along with prompts to insert the disks. You can then execute the command by just typing the name of the batch file. If the name of the batch file is DIRLIST, you save at least ten keystrokes each time you use the command. Batch files can be very simple and great time savers. They can also be very complex, powerful programs.

▶ TUTORIAL

In this tutorial, you first execute a batch file on the *Student Resource Disk* and then use the COPY CON command to create your own. The batch file that you create stores the directory of a disk in drive A into a disk file and then copies that file to the printer.

GETTING STARTED

1. Load DOS so that the command prompt is displayed.
2. Insert the disk labeled *Resource Disk—Backup* into drive A and make that the default drive.

EXECUTING A BATCH FILE

3. Type **README** and press [Enter←] to execute the batch file named README.BAT, which displays a box on the screen.

DISPLAYING THE CONTENTS OF A BATCH FILE

4. Type **TYPE README.BAT** and press [Enter←] to display the contents of the README.BAT file—the commands that are executed whenever you type the name of the batch file.
   - ECHO OFF prevents commands from being displayed on the screen as they are executed.

- CLS clears the screen.
- TYPE README.TXT displays the contents of the file named README.TXT.

CREATING A BATCH FILE

5. Type **COPY CON DIRLIST.BAT** and press [Enter ←].
6. Enter the text and commands shown in the figure "The DIRLIST.BAT Batch File." Two versions are shown, a long and a short. Since each line of the file must be perfect before you press [F6] to end it, you have to start over if you make a mistake. If you are having problems entering the long version, enter the shorter version. When entering either version:

The DIRLIST.BAT Batch File
You use the COPY CON command to enter the long or short version of this batch file in this tutorial. Both versions accomplish the same task, but the longer version displays more prompts.

```
CLS
ECHO Check that the printer is on!!
ECHO And that the disk in drive A is not write-protected!
PAUSE
CLS
ECHO These files are now being added to the DIRLIST.TXT file:
A:
DIR A:/W
DIR A: >A:\DIRLIST.TXT
COPY A:DIRLIST.TXT PRN
ERASE A:DIRLIST.TXT
ECHO All done!
ECHO You may have to advance the paper out of the printer.
```

Long Version

```
A:
DIR A:/W
DIR A: >A:\DIRLIST.TXT
COPY A:DIRLIST.TXT PRN
ERASE A:DIRLIST.TXT
```

Short Version

- Proofread each line carefully when you have finished typing it; once you have gone to the next line, you can't go back.
- Press [Enter ←] after entering each line but the last.
- After typing the last line, do not press [Enter ←]. Instead, press [F6] or [Ctrl]-[Z] to end the batch file, and a ^Z then appears on the screen. Press [Enter ←] to save the file. The drive spins as the file is saved onto the disk, and then the command prompt reappears.

7. Type **TYPE DIRLIST.BAT** and press [Enter ←] to display the contents of the batch file.

EXECUTING A BATCH FILE

8. Type **DIRLIST** and press [Enter ←] to execute the batch file.
   - If you entered the short version, your directory listing will immediately print out.
   - If you entered the long version, the messages that you entered following the ECHO commands are displayed, and the prompt reads *Press any key to continue*. Follow the instructions displayed on the screen, and then press any key.

9. Either continue to the next activity or quit for the day.

> **QUICK REFERENCE**

To create a batch file, you can use a word processing program that allows you to save files in ASCII text format, or you can use the DOS COPY CON command or DOS 5's EDIT command.

1. Load the operating system so that the command prompt is displayed on the screen. (If you are creating the batch file on a floppy disk, insert the program disk on which you want to create a batch file into drive A.) Make the drive on which you are creating the file the default drive.

2. Type **COPY CON** then the drive, then the name of the batch file (it must always have the extension .BAT), and then press [Enter ←]. The COPY CON command tells the computer to copy anything you type on the keyboard (console) to the specified file. The filename specification, for example, A:WP51.BAT, indicates the drive and file that the commands you type are copied to.

3. Type in the commands you want executed, just as you would normally enter them from the keyboard. End each command but the last by pressing [Enter ←].

4. When you have finished entering commands, press [F6] (or [Ctrl]-[Z]). This displays a ^Z on the screen.

5. Press [Enter ←] to save the file, and the drive spins. In a moment, the command prompt reappears. You can now execute the batch file by typing its name (without the extension) and pressing [Enter ←].

Batch files can contain text or commands. In the simplest form, the commands are just a list of program names or DOS commands. For example, you can create a batch file named WP51.BAT that automatically changes to the directory that contains WordPerfect and then executes the program. However, you can also use special commands to make your batch files more powerful. The table "Basic Batch File Commands" describes some typical commands.

TIPS

■ You cannot use a DOS program's name for a batch file because the operating system executes programs before it executes batch files with the same name. You can use the name of a program only if you put the batch file and program in separate directories or on separate disks. Even if you put them in separate directories, however, you may have problems depending on your system's PATH command.

■ To display or print the contents of a batch file, use the TYPE or PRINT command.

BASIC BATCH FILE COMMANDS

Command	Description
ECHO ON	Allows commands being executed to be displayed on the screen.
ECHO OFF	Prevents commands being executed from being displayed on the screen.
ECHO <message>	Displays a message on the screen.
PAUSE	Pauses a batch file and displays the prompt *Strike a key when ready.* (When you press any key, the batch file continues.)
REM <text>	(For "remark") Typed at the beginning of a line that is not to be executed—used, for example, to remind yourself what the file does.

EXERCISE 1

CREATING A BATCH FILE

```
DIR *.* >LIST.TXT
TYPE LIST.TXT
```

The LIST.BAT Batch File
You enter the batch file shown in this figure in this exercise.

1. Create on the *Resource Disk—Backup* the file shown in the figure "The LIST.BAT Batch File." Name it LIST.BAT.

2. Execute the batch file, and describe what each command does.

Special DOS Files

After completing this topic, you will be able to:
- Describe the functions of the CONFIG.SYS file
- Describe the functions of the AUTOEXEC.BAT file

When you boot the computer, it always takes a few moments for the command prompt, Shell, or a custom menu to appear on the screen. During this pause, the computer is very busy.

1. The computer first executes a small diagnostic program that is permanently stored in its read-only memory (ROM). This program checks the computer's memory to make certain it is operating correctly. If the computer finds a problem, it displays a message on the screen indicating where the problem is located and then stops.

2. If the diagnostic program finds no problems, the program in ROM executes two hidden operating system programs on the disk in the startup drive (named IBMBIO.COM and IBMDOS.COM on IBM versions of DOS). If the disk does not have the two system files (which are put on the disk when it is formatted), the computer displays an error message and stops.

3. Once the two operating system programs are executed, the computer looks for a program called COMMAND.COM, which contains the most frequently used internal operating system commands. Executing this program loads a copy of it into RAM, where it remains as long as the computer has power.

4. The computer then looks for a configuration file named CONFIG.SYS. This file contains commands that customize the system.

5. The computer next looks on the disk for a batch file named AUTOEXEC.BAT. If this file is present, the computer executes whatever commands are listed there. (On some older systems, you are then asked to enter the date and time.) The process is now complete. The screen display depends on the operating system you are using and the contents of the AUTOEXEC.BAT file.

▶ TUTORIAL

In this tutorial, you display and print your system's CONFIG.SYS and AUTOEXEC.BAT files if it has them.

GETTING STARTED

1. Load DOS so that the command prompt is displayed.
2. On a floppy disk system, insert your startup disk into drive A.
3. Set your drives as follows:
   - On a hard disk system, make drive C the default drive.
   - On a floppy disk system, make drive A the default drive.
4. Be sure that your printer is on.

DISPLAYING AND PRINTING YOUR SYSTEM'S CONFIG.SYS FILE

5. Type **TYPE CONFIG.SYS** and press [Enter←].
   - If your startup disk contains a CONFIG.SYS file, it is displayed on the screen.
   - If the message reads *File not found*, your system doesn't have the file. Proceed to Step 7.
6. If your system has a CONFIG.SYS file, type **COPY CONFIG.SYS PRN** and press [Enter←] to print it out.

DISPLAYING AND PRINTING YOUR SYSTEM'S AUTOEXEC.BAT FILE

7. Type **TYPE AUTOEXEC.BAT** and press [Enter←].
   - If your startup disk contains an AUTOEXEC.BAT file, it is displayed on the screen.
   - If the message reads *File not found*, your system doesn't have the file. Proceed to Step 9.
8. If your system has an AUTOEXEC.BAT file, type **COPY AUTOEXEC.BAT PRN** and press [Enter←] to print it out.

FINISHING UP

9. Either continue to the next activity or quit for the day.

> ## QUICK REFERENCE

When you first turn on your computer, it looks on the system disk in the startup drive for files named CONFIG.SYS and AUTOEXEC.BAT and executes the commands that are contained in those files.

CONFIG.SYS Files

CONFIG.SYS is called a configuration file because it stores commands that "configure" or set up your system. By changing the commands stored in this file, you can change the way your system operates. For example, many application programs work better and faster when there are BUFFERS and FILES statements in the CONFIG.SYS file. The table "Typical CONFIG.SYS Commands" describes these and other commands frequently used in CONFIG.SYS files.

A Typical CONFIG.SYS File
A typical CONFIG.SYS file might contain some or all of commands shown here.

```
DEVICE=C:\DOS\EGA.SYS
DEVICE=C:\QEMM\QEMM386.SYS RAM
DEVICE=C:\QEMM\LOADHI.SYS /R:2 /RES=13776 /SQF RCD.SYS /F /P
DOS=HIGH
DEVICEHIGH=DASDDRVR.SYS
BREAK=ON
BUFFERS=20
SHELL=C:\DOS\COMMAND.COM C:\DOS\ /E:256 /p
DEVICE=C:\WINDOWS\MOUSE.SYS /Y
DEVICE=C:\WINDOWS\SMARTDRV.EXE /DOUBLE_BUFFER
LASTDRIVE=Z
```

TYPICAL CONFIG.SYS COMMANDS

Command	Description
BUFFERS=<#>	Sets the number of disk buffers used by the system.
FILES=<#>	Sets the number of files that can be opened at one time.
LASTDRIVE=<drive>	Sets the maximum number of drives that can be addressed; for example, LASTDRIVE=B means you can address only drives A and B.
COUNTRY=<country>	Sets the country for keyboards and other country-dependent information, such as date formats.
DEVICE=<name>	Loads the specified device driver so that the device works with your system. For example, if you are using a mouse, your file may have a line such as DEVICE=MOUSE.SYS /Y.

AUTOEXEC Files

You use the AUTOEXEC.BAT file to store all commands that you want executed every time you turn on the computer. A typical AUTOEXEC.BAT file on a hard disk system might contain some or all of the commands shown in the figure "A Typical AUTOEXEC.BAT File." You could enter these commands from the keyboard each time you turn on the computer, but that would require 75 keystrokes. You can replace these keystrokes with a single AUTOEXEC file that automatically executes these commands when you turn on the computer. The AUTOEXEC.BAT file shown in the figure contains these commands:

A Typical AUTOEXEC.BAT File
A typical AUTOEXEC.BAT file might contain some or all of the commands shown here.

```
ECHO OFF
PATH C:\;C:\DOS;C:\123;C:\WP51;C:\DBASE
PROMPT $P$G
CLS
DIR *.BAT
```

- The *ECHO OFF* command prevents commands being executed from being displayed on the screen.
- The *PATH* command tells the computer which directories and subdirectories to look into (and in what order to do the looking) to find a command you execute that is not in the current default directory. It lays out a list of directories for the computer to search for a program, and the order in which to search them, so you don't have to change to the directory that contains a program to run it. Note how the specified directories are separated from one another by semicolons. (You can enter a PATH command from the command prompt by typing **PATH** followed by the directories you want searched. For example, to list directories named DOS, WP51, 123, and dBASE, you would type **PATH C:\;C:\DOS;C:\WP51;C:\123;C:\DBASE** and press (Enter⏎).
- The *PROMPT PG* command sets the prompt so that it displays the current directory followed by a greater-than sign.
- The *CLS* command clears the screen.
- The *DIR *.BAT* command displays a list of all batch files in the root directory. This is useful if you have a number of batch files that automatically load your programs and you would like to be reminded of their names.

Creating or Editing AUTOEXEC.BAT and CONFIG.SYS Files

If your system does not have an AUTOEXEC.BAT or CONFIG.SYS file, you can easily create them with the EDLIN program or DOS 5's EDIT program (see your DOS manual) or with any word processing program that allows you to save and retrieve ASCII text files. You can also create them from the command prompt using the COPY CON command. This command has very limited editing procedures, so you can correct errors only on the current line. If you notice a mistake on a previous line, you have to press (F6) and then (Enter⏎) to close the file. Then, you can reenter the file correctly.

Since these two files are important, you should not edit them unless you are sure of what you are doing. Before editing or revising either, you should make a backup copy of the original version so that you can recover it if something goes wrong. A good way to back it up is to copy it and change its name to AUTOEXEC.OLD or CONFIG.OLD. Before doing so, use the command DIR AUTOEXEC.* or CONFIG.* to see what versions already exist. When you install many application programs, they revise these files and rename the old file with a new extension. If anything goes wrong with the new version, you can just rename the backup file so that it has its original name.

Creating an AUTOEXEC.BAT or CONFIG.SYS File

1. Load the operating system so that the command prompt is displayed on the screen.
2. If you are creating the batch file on a floppy disk, insert the application program disk you want to create a batch file on into drive A.
3. Make the drive on which you are creating the file the default drive.
4. Type **COPY CON AUTOEXEC.BAT** or **COPY CON CONFIG.SYS** and press [Enter←┘].
5. Type in the commands you want executed just as you would normally enter them from the keyboard. Press [Enter←┘] after entering each command except the last.
6. When you are finished entering commands, press [F6] and a ^Z is displayed.
7. Press [Enter←┘] to save the file and return to the command prompt.
8. You can now execute the batch file by typing its name and pressing [Enter←┘] or by booting the computer with the disk containing the AUTOEXEC.BAT or CONFIG.SYS file in the startup drive. On the IBM PC and compatible computers, you can press [Ctrl]-[Alt]-[Del] to warm-boot the system if it is already running.

► E X E R C I S E

EXERCISE 1

CREATING AN AUTOEXEC.BAT FILE

1. Insert your *Resource Disk—Backup* into drive A and make that the default drive. (Be sure drive C isn't the default drive on a hard disk system or you'll overwrite the existing AUTOEXEC.BAT file.
2. Create the following AUTOEXEC.BAT file:

```
PROMPT $P$G
DIR
```

3. Make a printout of the file.

Using the DOS 5 Shell

After completing this topic, you will be able to:
- Describe the parts of the DOS Shell
- Use DOS Shell menus to execute commands

DOS 5 contains a built-in Shell that gives you a visual representation of the drives, directories, and files on your system as shown in the figure "The DOS 5 Shell." You can select any of these items and then execute the most frequently used DOS commands on them by making choices from menus like the one shown in the figure "The Shell's Pull-Down Menus." You can also list your own application programs on the Shell's program list so that you can run them directly from the Shell.

The DOS 5 Shell
The DOS 5 Shell contains all the elements shown in this figure. However, your screen display may differ from the MS-DOS 5 shell shown here. The Shell can be displayed in character or graphics mode, and the areas shown and the programs listed can be modified. There are also differences between the MS-DOS and IBM-DOS versions of the Shell.

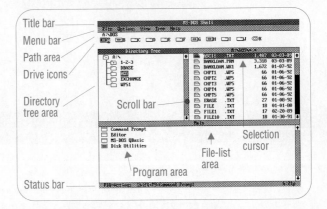

The Shell's screen display is divided into a number of areas, each of which displays a different type of information.

- The *path area* lists the current default path. For example, when it reads *C:*, the current directory is the root directory on drive C. If it reads *C:\DOS*, then DOS is the current directory.
- The *drive icon area* indicates the drives on your system with graphic symbols, called icons. The icon for the current default drive is always highlighted.
- The *directory-tree area* lists directories and subdirectories on the disk in the default drive. The current directory is always highlighted.
- The *file-list area* lists the files in the current directory. When you change the current directory on the directory tree, or select another drive in the drive-icon area, the list of files automatically changes.
- The *program-list area* lists programs that you can run without leaving the Shell.

In addition to these areas, the Shell displays the following items:

- The *menu bar* lists the names of menus that you can pull down to display commands.
- The *selection cursor* is a reverse-video or colored highlight that you move among areas of the screen to select drives, directories, files, or program names.
- A *mouse pointer* is displayed if your system has a mouse and DOS has been set up for it.
- The *status bar* lists messages and keys you can press to execute commands.

The Shell's Pull-Down Menus
When you press [Alt] or click on the menu bar with the mouse pointer, you can pull down menus listing many DOS commands.

> **T U T O R I A L**

In this tutorial, you use the Shell that is built into DOS 5. As you do so, you select commands from the keyboard, not with a mouse. If your system has a mouse, you can repeat the tutorial using the mouse instead of the keyboard to execute commands.

GETTING STARTED

1. Load DOS so that the Shell is displayed. If the Shell is not displayed automatically:
   - On a hard disk system, type **DOSSHELL** and press [Enter ←].
   - On a floppy disk system, insert the disk that contains the Shell program into drive A, type **DOSSHELL** and press [Enter ←].
2. Insert your disks as follows:
   - On a hard disk system, insert the disk labeled *Resource Disk— Backup* into drive A.
   - On a floppy disk system, insert the disk labeled *Resource Disk— Backup* into drive B.

CHANGING DEFAULT DRIVES

3. Press [→] to move the selection cursor from drive icon to drive icon. (If the selection cursor is not in the drive-icon area of the screen, press [Tab ⇆] one or more times to move it there.)
4. Select one of the drive icons as follows:

- On a hard disk system, highlight the icon for drive A and press Enter↵.
- On a floppy disk system, highlight the icon for drive B and press Enter↵.

EXPLORING HELP

5. Press Alt to select the menu bar, and the first letter in each menu name is highlighted.

6. Press H (for **H**elp), and the Help menu descends from the menu bar.

7. Press S (for **S**hell Basics), and a help panel appears that describes Shell basics.

8. Press ↓ or PgDn to scroll down through the help text, and press ↑ or PgUp to scroll back up. Additional topics on which you can display help are highlighted in color or reverse video.

9. Press ↓ or ↑ to display the list of related help topics. The first topic listed is *Welcome to MS-DOS Shell* (or *Welcome to IBM DOS Shell* on the IBM version of DOS).

10. Press Tab↹ repeatedly to move the selection cursor to the *Index* command button at the bottom of the help window, and press Enter↵ to display an index of help topics.

11. Scroll through the list, highlight any topic of interest, and press Enter↵ to display help on it.

12. Continue exploring help until you are comfortable with how it works.

13. When you have finished exploring help, press Esc to remove the help panel and return to the Shell.

EXPLORING MENUS WITH ARROW KEYS

14. Press Alt to activate the menu bar, and the File menu's name is highlighted.

15. Press ↓ to pull down the File menu, and all available commands are listed.

16. Press → to pull down the Options menu.

17. Press → to pull down the View menu.

18. Press → to pull down the Tree menu.

19. Press → to pull down the Help menu.

20. Press → to pull down the File menu again.

21. Press ↓ to highlight *Create directory*, and press Enter↵ to display a dialog box with a space into which you type the name of the new directory.

22. Type **MYDIR** and press Enter↵ to add a new directory named MYDIR to the menu tree.

EXPLORING MENUS WITH MNEMONIC KEYS

23. Press Tab↹ to move the selection cursor to the Directory Tree and highlight *MYDIR* directory.

24. Press Alt and then F (for **F**ile) to pull down the File menu.

25. Press ⟦D⟧ (for **D**elete) to remove the highlighted directory from the disk and the directory tree. If the confirmation on delete option is on, a prompt reads *Delete A:\MYDIR?* or *Delete B:\MYDIR?*. If this prompt appears, highlight *Yes* and press ⟦Enter ←⟧.

RENAMING A FILE

26. Press ⟦Tab ⇆⟧ to move the section cursor to the File list.
27. Highlight the file named *WHATSUP.DOC*.
28. Press ⟦Alt⟧ to select the menu bar.
29. Press ⟦F⟧ (for **F**ile) to pull down the File menu.
30. Press ⟦N⟧ (for Re**n**ame) to display a dialog box.
31. Type **NEWFILE.DOC** and press ⟦Enter ←⟧ to change the file's name on the File list to NEWFILE.DOC.

COPYING A FILE

32. Highlight the file named NEWFILE.DOC, and press ⟦Alt⟧ to select the menu bar.
33. Press ⟦F⟧ (for **F**ile) to pull down the File menu.
34. Press ⟦C⟧ (for **C**opy) to display a dialog box.
35. Type **WHATSUP.DOC** and press ⟦Enter ←⟧ to add the filename WHATSUP.DOC to the File list.

ERASING A FILE

36. Highlight the file named *NEWFILE.DOC*.
37. Press ⟦Alt⟧ to select the menu bar.
38. Press ⟦F⟧ (for **F**ile) to pull down the File menu.
39. Press ⟦D⟧ (for **D**elete) to delete the highlighted file from the disk and remove it from the file list. If the confirmation on delete option is on, a prompt reads *Delete A:\NEWFILE.DOC?* or *Delete B:\NEWFILE.DOC?*. If this prompt appears, highlight *Yes* and press ⟦Enter ←⟧.

FINISHING UP

40. Either continue to the next activity or quit for the day.

▶ Q U I C K   R E F E R E N C E

You can execute the Shell's commands with the keyboard or with a mouse. When doing so, you can display help at any time.

Getting Help

Whenever the Shell is displayed, you can display help by pressing ⟦F1⟧ or by pulling down the Help menu and selecting a topic. Help is context sensitive, which means the help text displayed (called a help panel) depends on the cursor's position. Many help panels have lists of related commands displayed in color or reverse video. You press ⟦Tab ⇆⟧ to move a highlight or a small arrow from one of these topics to another. With the topic highlighted or with the small arrow pointing to it, press ⟦Enter ←⟧

to display help on it. To remove the help panel, press Esc. At the bottom of each help panel are command buttons that close the help window, move you back, display help on keys, show an index, or display help on help. To choose one of these, press Tab⇆ to move the selection cursor to the desired button, and press Enter ↵. If you are using a mouse, you can click on topics or command buttons to choose them. To do so, you use the mouse to move the mouse pointer on the screen. When the mouse pointer is pointing to the desired topic or button, you click the left button.

The Help System
You can press F1 at any point, and help is displayed on the screen. You can use the arrow keys to scroll through the text or select other related help topics that are highlighted.

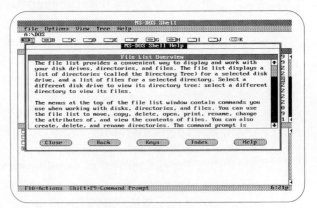

Moving Between Areas of the Shell

When the Shell is loaded, the screen displays the DOS Shell window. This window is divided into a number of areas, each of which displays a different type of information. The areas include those that display drive icons, a directory tree, a file list, and a program list. Commands listed on the View menu govern which of these areas is displayed on your system.

- You move the selection cursor between areas by pressing Tab⇆ or **Backtab**. (Hold down ⇧ Shift and press Tab⇆.)
- You move within areas by pressing the arrow keys.

Using the Shell's Pull-Down Menus

The menu bar contains pull-down menus with the choices listed in the table "The DOS Shell Menu Choices." (The choices on the File menu are different when the selection cursor is in the Program list.)

- To activate and deactivate the menu bar, you press Alt or F10. Once the menu is activated, press → or ← to move between menu choices and then press ↓ to pull down the highlighted menu. You can then press → or ← to pull down other menus.
- If using a mouse, you point to the menu name, and then click to pull it down. The mouse pointer is displayed as a highlighted box (in text mode) or as an arrow (in graphics mode). If you pull down a menu and decide not to make a choice, point to any area outside the menu, and then click the mouse button. The table "Executing Commands with a Mouse" describes the procedures you follow to execute commands with a mouse.

EXECUTING COMMANDS WITH A MOUSE

To	Point To	Click
Pull down a menu	Menu's name	Left button
Start a program	Program's name	Left button twice
Exit a pull-down menu without making a choice	Outside menu	Left button

When the menu bar is activated, you can pull down the menus in three ways:

■ By pressing the letter that is underlined or highlighted (called a mnemonic) in the choice's name. For example, you can press $\boxed{F}$ to pull down the File menu or $\boxed{H}$ to pull down the Help menu.
■ By using the arrow keys to highlight the name with the selection cursor and pressing $\boxed{\text{Enter} \leftarrow}$ or $\boxed{\downarrow}$ to pull down the menu.
■ By clicking on the desired menu name with a mouse.

If you do not want to make a selection, press $\boxed{\text{Esc}}$ or point with the mouse to another area of the screen and click.

The table "Executing Commands from the Keyboard" summarizes the keys you use to execute menu commands.

EXECUTING COMMANDS FROM THE KEYBOARD

To	Press
Activate or deactivate the menu bar	$\boxed{\text{Alt}}$ or $\boxed{\text{F10}}$
Pull down a menu from the activated menu bar	
with arrow keys	$\boxed{\leftarrow}$ or $\boxed{\rightarrow}$ and then $\boxed{\downarrow}$
with mnemonic keys	Mnemonic letter
Select a choice from a pull-down menu	
with arrow keys	$\boxed{\downarrow}$ or $\boxed{\uparrow}$ and then $\boxed{\text{Enter} \leftarrow}$
with mnemonic keys	Mnemonic letter
Exit a pull-down menu without making a choice but leave the menu bar activated	$\boxed{\text{Alt}}$ or $\boxed{\text{F10}}$
Exit a pull-down menu without making a choice and deactivate the menu bar	$\boxed{\text{Esc}}$
Move the selection cursor between areas of the Shell	$\boxed{\text{Tab} \leftrightarrows}$

The choices on the menu bar provide additional information other than the command they execute.

■ Choices on pull-down menus followed by an ellipsis (...) display dialog boxes when selected. Dialog boxes are like on-screen forms that you fill out with information the computer needs.
■ Choices on pull-down menus that are dimmed or not listed are not selectable from where you are in the procedure.

THE DOS SHELL MENU CHOICES

Menu	Description
File	
Open	Runs the selected executable program file that ends with the extension .COM, .EXE, or .BAT and opens an associated file if you selected one (see **A**ssociate).
Run...	Displays a dialog box in which you enter the name of a program you want to run.
Print	Prints up to ten selected ASCII text files.
Associate...	Links filename extension to programs so that if you select a data file with the specified extension, the associated program is automatically run.
Search...	Searches for files that you specify in a dialog box that appears when you select this choice. If you check the Search entire disk option, DOS searches the disk in the default drive. If you leave this unchecked, DOS just searches the current directory.
View File Contents	Displays the contents of the selected file.
Move...	Moves selected files to another drive or directory and deletes the original file.
Copy...	Copies selected files to another drive or directory or to the current one if you specify a new name in the dialog box.
Delete...	Deletes selected files.
Re**n**ame...	Renames selected files.
Change Attributes	Changes a selected file's attributes to Hidden, Read-Only, or Archive. (See your DOS manual.)
Create Directory...	Creates a new directory.
Select All	Selects all files in the File List.
Dese**l**ect All	Deselects any previously selected files in the File List.
Ex**i**t	Closes the Shell and displays the command prompt.
Options	
Confirmation...	Turns confirmation prompts on and off for **D**elete, **C**opy, and **M**ove commands; also specifies if files are to be selected in more than one directory or not.
File Display Options...	Displays selected files and sorts files in the File List.
Select **A**cross Directories...	Allows you to select files in more than one directory at the same time so that you can copy, move, or delete them.
Show Information...	Displays information on the highlighted file.
Enable Task Swapper	When enabled, you can run more than one program at the same time and switch back and forth between them.
Display...	Changes the way the Shell is displayed.
Co**l**ors...	Changes the colors used in the Shell display.
View	
Single File List	Displays Directory Tree and File List for current drive.
Dual File Lists	Displays Directory Tree and File List for two drives or directories.
All Files	Displays a list of all files on a disk regardless of the directories they are stored in.
Program/**F**ile Lists	Displays Directory Tree and File List for current drive and a list of DOS programs.
Program List	Displays just a list of DOS programs.

Menu	Description
*Re*paint Screen	Updates the screen display.
*R*efresh	Updates the list of files after you delete or restore any.
Tree	
Expand One Level	Shows one more level of subdirectories for the selected directory.
Expand Branch	Shows all levels of subdirectories for the selected directory.
Expand *A*ll	Shows all levels of subdirectories for all directories.
Collapse Branch	Hides all subdirectories below the selected directory.
Help	
*I*ndex	Displays a list of topics on which help is available.
*K*eyboard	Displays a list of topics on keys you use to execute commands.
*S*hell Basics	Displays basic help on using the Shell.
*C*ommands	Displays all menu commands so that you can get help on them.
*P*rocedures	Displays a list of procedures you may need help with.
*U*sing Help	Displays help on using help.
*A*bout Shell	Displays the version number and copyright information on the Shell.

Responding to Dialog Boxes

All menu choices followed by an ellipsis (...) display dialog boxes when you select them. Dialog boxes are requests for additional information, which you enter into the dialog boxes' text boxes or select from lists. When the text that you type into a text box reaches the right end of the box, the entry scrolls off the screen to the left. If your entry is too long, eventually the computer beeps, and you have to stop typing.

When entering text into text boxes, you can use the following editing commands:

- You can press [←] and [→] to move the cursor through the text. You can also press [End] to move the cursor to the end of the entry or [Home] to move it to the beginning.
- If the text box already contains an entry, the first character you type will delete it. If you want to just edit the existing entry, press [←] or [→] before typing any other character, and you will enter edit mode. In this mode, you can then move the cursor through the entry to insert characters or use [Del] or [←Bksp] to delete them.

Changing Default Drives

The drive-icon area lists the drives on your system. The current default drive is highlighted. To change the default drive:

- Press [Tab↹] to move the selection cursor to this area, press [←] or [→] to highlight the drive you want to make the default, and press [Enter←]. You can also hold down [Ctrl] and press the letter of the drive when the selection cursor is in the drive-icon area.
- If using a mouse, point to the drive and then click.

As you change the default drive, the path area, the directory tree, and the file list reflect the change.

Changing Default Directories

The directory-tree area lists all directories and subdirectories, if any, on the disk. To change the default directory:

- Press [Tab⇆] to move the selection cursor to this area, press [↓] or [↑] to highlight the directory you want to make the default, and press [Enter ↵].
- If using a mouse, point to the directory, and then click.

As you change the default directory, the path area and file list reflect the change.

Selecting Files

The file-list area normally lists the files on the default drive and directory. At the top of this area the current file specification is listed. You can change this specification with the *File Display Options* command listed on the Options menu. The default file specification is *.* which displays all the files on the disk.

- If there are too many filenames to be displayed at one time, the list extends off the bottom of the area. To scroll through the list of files, press [Tab⇆] to move the selection cursor to this area. You then press [↑], [↓], [PgUp], and [PgDn] to scroll the list. You can also press [Ctrl]-[Home] to move to the top of the list or [Ctrl]-[End] to move to the bottom.
- To select a single file, press [⇧ Shift]-[F8], and *ADD* is displayed on the status bar and the file's icon remains highlighted when you move the selection cursor off it. To unselect a selected file, highlight the file, and press [Spacebar].
- To select files that are adjacent to one another on the list, you select the first filename, and then extend the selection. To do so, highlight the first file you want to select, and then hold down [⇧ Shift] while you press [↑] or [↓] to extend the selection to the other files.
- To select or deselect files that are not adjacent to one another, highlight the first file, and press [⇧ Shift]-[F8]. When you do so, *ADD* is displayed on the status bar, and the file's icon remains highlighted when you move the selection cursor off it. To select additional files, highlight them and press [Spacebar]. After selecting all the files you want, press [⇧ Shift]-[F8] again, and *ADD* disappears from the status bar.
- To select or deselect all files, press [Tab⇆] to move the selection cursor to the file-list area, pull down the File menu, and then choose **S**elect all or *Deselect all*.

If your Shell has been installed for a mouse, the arrows or scroll bar can be used instead of [PgUp] and [PgDn] to scroll the file list or directory tree. The scroll bar contains both up and down arrows and a slider box. The slider box indicates which part of the list is currently displayed. To scroll any list:

- Point to the arrows at the top or bottom of the scroll bar, and then click. Hold the mouse button down to scroll continuously.

- Point to the slider box within the scroll bar, hold down the mouse button, and drag the slider box up or down. Release the button to scroll the list to that point.
- To select files that are adjacent to one another on the list, click the first name, and then hold down ⇧Shift and click the last name.
- To select or deselect files that are not adjacent to one another, hold down Ctrl while you click each filename.

Running Programs

A program list is displayed when you select *Program/File Lists* from the View menu. This area lists programs that you can execute. Some programs are directly listed in this area, but others have been grouped together under a single heading. For example, if you select *Command Prompt* or *Editor* (called *IBM DOS Editor* on IBM's version of DOS 5), the command is immediately executed. However, if you select *Disk Utilities*, another list is displayed. It is from this second list that you actually execute the commands.

The default program list (yours may have been modified) is named Main, and it contains those programs shown in the table "The Program-List Area Commands." To select one of the listed commands, highlight it and press Enter↵ or double-click it with a mouse. (Click on it twice in rapid succession.)

THE PROGRAM-LIST AREA COMMANDS FOR MS-DOS (DIFFERENT ON IBM VERSION)

Choice	Description
Command Prompt	Displays the command prompt. Type **EXIT** and press Enter↵ to return to the Shell.
Editor	Displays a dialog box asking you the name of the file that you want to edit.
MS-DOS QBasic	Displays a dialog box asking you the name of the file that you want to run.
Disk Utilities	Displays a list of utility programs you can run. • *Main* returns you to the main program list. • *Disk Copy* makes duplicate disks. • *Backup Fixed Disk* backs up a hard disk onto floppy disks. • *Restore Fixed Disk* restores a hard disk's files from backups on floppy disks. • *Quick Format* formats a disk more quickly if it has already been formatted once. • *Format* formats data and system disks. • *Undelete* recovers deleted files.

When the selection cursor is in the program-list area, the commands listed on the File menu change from those that are normally displayed. These commands are described in the table "File Menu Choices with the Selection Cursor in the Program List."

FILE MENU CHOICES WITH THE SELECTION CURSOR IN THE PROGRAM LIST

Choice	Description
*N*ew...	Adds a program or group of programs to the currently selected group
*O*pen	Runs a program or displays the contents of a group
*C*opy	Copies a program or group of programs to another group
*D*elete...	Deletes the selected group or selected item within a group
*P*roperties...	Describes the program to be run
*Re*order	Rearranges programs and groups to a different position in the list
*R*un...	Displays a dialog box in which you enter the name of a program to run
E*x*it	Closes the Shell and displays the command prompt

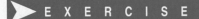

E X E R C I S E

EXERCISE 1

USING THE SHELL'S MENUS

1. Insert your *Resource Disk—Backup* into drive A on a hard disk system or drive B on a floppy disk system.
2. Change the default drive, if necessary, to the drive into which you inserted the disk.
3. Use the Shell's menus to create three directories, SHELL1, SHELL2, and SHELL3.
4. Use the Shell's menus to copy all the files that begin with CHPT to the SHELL1 directory.
5. Use the Shell's menus to copy all the files that begin with FILE to the SHELL2 directory.
6. Use the Shell's menus to copy the WHATSUP.DOC file to the SHELL3 directory.
7. Use the Shell's menus to erase all the files in each directory, and then delete the directories.

REVIEW

- The command you use to check your disks is CHKDSK, an external command. When files are deleted and then new files are saved onto a disk, files that you copy to the disk or save onto it with an application program may be stored in noncontiguous sectors. To find files like this, use the CHKDSK *.* command.
- The command you use to display an ASCII text file on the screen is TYPE. To freeze a file scrolling on the screen, press [Ctrl]-[S]. To resume scrolling, press any other key.
- The command you use to print an ASCII text file is PRINT, an external command. To stop a file being printed with this command, use the PRINT/T command.
- The > character is used to redirect a file to a disk file or the printer. The >> characters append a file to an existing disk file.
- The MORE command pauses data on the screen if the screen becomes full. You then have to press any key to continue.
- The SORT command sorts files and their contents.
- To create a batch file from the command prompt, you use the COPY CON command, an internal command. To end it, you press [Ctrl]-[Z], and then press [Enter←].
- When you first boot your system, the computer looks for two files, CONFIG.SYS and AUTOEXEC.BAT. It automatically executes the commands that it finds in these files.
- Because DOS commands can be hard to remember, Shells have been developed that allow you to execute DOS commands by making menu selections. You can display DOS 4 and later Shells by typing **DOSSHELL** at the command prompt.

QUESTIONS

FILL IN THE BLANK

1. To check the disk in drive A, you would enter the command _____.

2. To display an ASCII text file named README.TXT, you would enter the command _____.

3. To print an ASCII text file named README.TXT, you would enter the command _____.

4. To stop printing an ASCII text file that is being printed with the PRINT command, you would enter the command _____.

5. To pause a directory listing for drive C that is listed with the DIR command, you would enter the command _____.

6. To send a directory listing of drive B to the printer, you would enter the command _____.

7. To send a directory listing of drive B to a disk file on drive A named LIST.TXT, you would enter the command _____.

8. To create a batch file named BATCH.BAT, you would enter the command _____.

9. The file your system reads first when you boot it up is named _____.

10. The file your system reads next when you boot it up is named _____.

11. To load the DOS Shell from the command prompt, you would type _____.

MATCH THE COLUMNS

1. CHKDSK
2. CHKDSK *.*
3. CHKDSK /V
4. CHKDSK /F
5. TYPE
6. PRINT
7. >
8. >>
9. | MORE
10. | SORT
11. COPY CON
12. F6
13. CONFIG.SYS
14. AUTOEXEC.BAT
15. DOSSHELL
16. Alt

__ Sorts files or their contents

__ Pauses the screen when it is full

__ Fixes a disk that has lost chains

__ Creates an ASCII text file

__ Prints ASCII text files

__ Gives you the status of a disk

__ Redirects data to a disk file or the printer

__ Activates the DOS Shell's menu bar

__ Gives you the status of a disk and the files on it

__ Displays the Shell built into DOS 4 and later versions

__ A file that contains information about your system's setup

__ Appends data to an existing disk file

__ A file that contains commands to be executed when you boot the computer

__ Lists files as it checks a disk's status

__ Displays ASCII text files on the screen

__ Ends an ASCII text file you are creating with COPY CON

WRITE OUT THE ANSWERS

1. What command do you use to check disks? Is the command an internal or external command?

2. What happens to files, when the disk begins to get full, that makes the drive work harder and take longer to retrieve and save the files?

3. If you get a message telling you your files have noncontiguous sectors, what does it mean?

4. If a disk has noncontiguous sectors, how can you fix the files so that they are all in adjacent sectors on the disk?

5. What is the difference between the CHKDSK and CHKDSK *.* commands?

6. What command do you use to display ASCII files on the screen? Is this an internal or external command?

7. What two commands can you use to stop text from scrolling off the screen?

8. To redirect the output from the standard output device, what redirection character do you use?

9. What is the function of a filter?

10. If you want to sort a file, what filter do you use?

11. What is the function of a pipe?

12. What character do you use to direct the list of files to the printer or a file?

13. What command would you use to redirect the output from the DIR command to the printer? To a file named FILELIST on a disk in drive B?

14. Why can't the disk in the default drive be write-protected when you use the MORE filter?

15. What are batch files, and what are they used for?

16. What is the command you type to begin creating a batch file from the command prompt?

17. What key(s) do you press to end a batch file and save it to the disk?

18. What command do you type to display the DOS Shell from the command prompt?

19. When the DOS Shell is displayed, what key do you press to activate the menu bar?

PROJECT

PROJECT 1

CREATING A DOS REFERENCE CARD

The table "Summary of DOS Commands" lists some of the most frequently used DOS command procedures. Complete the table by entering in the Command column the command you would use to perform each of the tasks. In the Type column, indicate if the command is an internal or external command.

SUMMARY OF DOS COMMANDS

Description	Command	Type
Checking Disks		
Gives status of memory, disk space, and any noncontiguous blocks	_____	_____
Displays each filename as it is checked	_____	_____
Displays a prompt that asks you if you want to correct errors	_____	_____
Displaying and Printing ASCII File Commands		
Displays ASCII text file on screen	_____	_____
Freezes scrolling screen display	_____	_____
Prints ASCII text file	_____	_____
Stops a printing ASCII text file	_____	_____
Batch File Commands		
Copies from console (keyboard) to disk file	_____	_____
Ends a COPY CON command	_____	_____

INDEX

Note: DOS commands are in **boldface**.

Checking Disks

Indicate status of memory and disk space	CHKDSK
Look for noncontiguous blocks	CHKDSK *.*
Fix lost clusters	CHKDSK /F

Displaying and Printing ASCII Text Files

Display ASCII text file	TYPE *<filename>*
Pause a file display	TYPE *<filename>* IMORE
Print an ASCII text file	PRINT *<filename>*
Print screen display from enhanced keyboard	**PrintScreen**
Print screen display from standard keyboard	Shift - PrtScr
Print all text as it appears on the screen	Ctrl - PrtScr
Turn off printing all text as it appears on the screen	Ctrl - PrtScr
Pause scrolling screen display	Ctrl - S or Pause

Creating and Using Batch Files

Create a batch file	COPY CON *<filename.bat>*
End a batch file	Ctrl - Z or F6
Display contents of a batch file	TYPE *<filename.bat>*
Edit a batch file (DOS 5 only)	EDIT *<filename.bat>*

Using the Shell (DOS 4 and 5 only)

Display the Shell	DOSSHELL
Activate the menu bar	F10 or Alt
Exit menus without making choice	Esc
Display help	F1
Move between areas of the Shell	Tab
Select files	Shift - F8 then Spacebar
Exit the DOS Shell	F3

DOS Pocket Guide

Basic Commands

Display the version of DOS in memory	VER
Display system date	DATE
Display system time	TIME
Change the prompt to display directories	PROMPT PG
Reboot the system	Ctrl - Alt - Del
Cancel a command in progress	Ctrl - Break
Display help index (DOS 5 only)	HELP
Display help on specific command (DOS 5 only)	HELP *<command>*
Load DOSKEY (DOS 5 only)	DOSKEY
Display all commands saved by DOSKEY	DOSKEY /HISTORY
Display last command saved by DOSKEY	↑

Changing the Default Drive

Make drive A the default drive	A:
Make drive B the default drive	B:
Make drive C the default drive	C:

Formatting Data Disks

Format a data disk	FORMAT *<drive:>*
Format a data disk w/volume name	FORMAT *<drive:>*/V
Load the MIRROR program (DOS 5 only)	MIRROR *<drive:>*
Unformat a disk (DOS 5 only)	UNFORMAT *<drive:>*
Label a formatted disk	LABEL *<drive:>*
Display volume label	VOL *<drive:>*

Formatting System Disks

Format disk as a system disk	FORMAT *<drive:>*/S
Format a system disk with a volume name	FORMAT *<drive:>*/S/V

Listing Files

List all files	DIR *<drive:>*
List all files in a directory	DIR *<drive:\directory>*
List files in five columns	DIR *<drive:>*/w
List files so screen pauses when full	DIR *<drive:>*/P
List files with specified filename	DIR *<drive:> <filename>*.*
List files with specified extension	DIR *<drive:>* *.*<ext>*
Wildcard that stands for a single character	?
Wildcard that stands for all characters to end of name or extension	*
Print directory listing	DIR *.* >PRN
Store directory listing in a disk file	DIR ><drive:/filename>
Pause a directory listing	DIR |MORE

Sorting Directories (second set of commands for DOS 5 only)

Sort directory by filename	DIR	SORT or DIR /ON
Sort directory by extension	DIR	SORT /+10 or DIR /OE
Sort directory by file size	DIR	SORT /+14 or DIR /OS
Sort directory by date	DIR	SORT /+24 or DIR /OD

Copying Files

Copy individual file from drive A to B	COPY A:*<filename>* B:
Copy all files from drive A to B	COPY A:*.* B
Copy all files from drive B to A	COPY B:*.* A

Duplicating Disks

Duplicate a disk in drive A to a disk in drive B	DISKCOPY A: B:

Comparing Disks

Compare a disk in drive A with a disk in drive B	DISKCOMP A: B:

Renaming Files

Rename a file	RENAME *<old name> <new name>*

Deleting Files

Delete file from disk	DEL *<filename>* or ERASE *<filename>*
Delete all files with the specified extension	ERASE *.*<ext>*
Delete all files with the specified filename	ERASE *<filename>*.*
Delete all files	ERASE *.*
Undelete files (DOS 5 only)	UNDELETE *<filename>*
List deleted files (DOS 5 only)	UNDELETE *<drive:>* /LIST
Mirror deleted files (DOS 5 only)	MIRROR/T*<drive:>*

Making Directories

Create new directory below current directory	MD *<directory name>*
Specify a path	*<drive:>\<directory>\<subdirectory>*

Removing Directories

Remove directory from current directory	RD *<directory name>*

Changing Directories

Change the default directory	CD *<directory name>*
Return to the root directory	CD\
Move up one directory level	CD ..
Display the default directory on another drive	CD *<drive:>*

Listing Directories

List directories	DIR *.
List directories	TREE *<drive:>*
List directories and files	TREE *<drive:>*/F